FROM THE VERY FIRST WORDS of this book, I was gripped. Ann Shakespeare's narrative of the crisis that engulfed Neville Jayaweera's professional life and reputation was so vivid that it drew me in. I was there in my imagination on his spiritual journey, his trying to find answers through Buddhist disciplines, and his totally unexpected encounter with the Spirit of Jesus Christ.

As an ecologist I was fascinated by the effect his new faith and life had on his relationship with the natural realm, including the stilling of a storm and the sight of wild, jungle-dwelling animals suddenly moving from fear to trust in his presence. And as a scientist I was intrigued and inspired by the way he later applied the principles of quantum physics to his understanding of spiritual truth, as he developed his discipline of meditation which nevertheless was "firmly grounded in biblical Scriptures."

This book provides an absorbing insight into the life of an extraordinary man and a deep well of spiritual teaching.

The Reverend Leslie Batty, priest, ecologist,
eco-theologian, and co-founder of A Rocha

ANN'S RELAXED AND FLUENT writing style puts you at ease and makes it easy to read this story of a remarkable Sri Lankan man of God, her dear friend and mentor, who inspired and mentored her to follow after Christ by the amazing example of his own life.

His understanding and experience of "gazing" upon the Lord, and meditating on His Word—until it becomes real in you—will both encourage and inspire you as it did me. This truth helped affirm what I already knew but realised as an all-important key I had to apply to gain victory in an area of my own life.

A Luminous Encounter will have a tremendous impact in people's lives, inspiring and helping many to pursue a deeper, more intimate and dependent walk with the Lord Jesus.

Lincoln Rupesinghe, co-founder of Rivers of Life Word Ministries

A LUMINOUS ENCOUNTER

THE LIFE AND TEACHINGS OF A REMARKABLE MAN OF GOD

ANN SHAKESPEARE

Deep River
BOOKS

DEDICATION

For my beloved Neville Jayaweera,
passionate lover of Jesus Christ,
the Father, and the Holy Spirit.

ACKNOWLEDGMENTS

NICHOLAS, MY EVER-SUPPORTIVE AND LOVING husband. Thank you for your wise discipline that held me on track, and for the tender hugs that kept me going along the way.

MY PRAYER PARTNERS AT HOME and around the world—you all know who you are. You are an absolute joy, and God's gift to me. I am forever grateful.

ALEXIS MILLER, MY EXTRAORDINARILY KIND and gifted editor. Thank you.

SARAH SHORE, THE TALENTED ARTIST who rendered a map of Sri Lanka (sarahshore.art@gmail.com).

CONTENTS

INTRODUCTION

THIS BOOK IS AN INVITATION to enter into encounter with God. Wherever you are in your life or in your spiritual walk, it is God's desire to draw you into ever-deeper relationship with Him through Jesus Christ. The cross speaks of our value to God and of His fervent love for each one of us. It strips away every barrier erected by the Fall and by sin, and invites every single person into fellowship with our Father. For Neville Jayaweera, this fellowship began when he experienced the presence of God in a way that he had never known before. In his diaries, he described it as a "luminous encounter," and it marked the beginning of radical internal and external changes in his life.

At that time, by the world's standards, he was a highly successful public servant. He filled prominent roles in his native Sri Lanka, including being placed in charge of a vast, multipurpose development project, then appointed to restructure and lead the national broadcasting corporation. But nothing could ease the ache in his heart for a much deeper Reality, until, in 1970, he met the One he had—unknowingly—been longing for all his life. It was Jesus Christ.

The effects were immediate and dramatic. He stepped out from the financial security of senior government employment and flew to the UK, with his wife and daughter, to accept a modest position with a small Christian charity in London. That was where I first met Neville in 1984—the start of our teacher-pupil relationship of almost forty years.

As we grew to know each other, I was drawn to him like a magnet. It wasn't just because he was gentle and kind, or because he had a delightful sense of humor, though both were true. At the time, in my spiritual immaturity, I couldn't really explain why. Now, in 2023, I look back and *can* see why—so very clearly. It was because Neville knew God with an intimacy that was absolutely compelling.

Brought up a practicing Buddhist, Neville had a luminous encounter with the Spirit of Jesus Christ while he was in charge of a national district at the time of a violent rebel uprising. In the midst of all the violence and the turmoil, Neville's conscious relationship with the Lord was born, and a lifetime of unbroken fellowship began.

Neville's conversion was particularly remarkable because he had not been seeking Jesus at all. Instead, not surprisingly, he had been searching for truth through his own cultural traditions. However, when he did begin to read the Bible, he found to his amazement that it described what was happening inside him. He realized that the humanly inexplicable qualities of love, peace, and joy that had literally enveloped him were indeed supernatural—they were gifts of the Holy Spirit!

When we met, Neville had walked with Jesus for ten years, and he already had a rich history of living in the Spirit. From early on, I was very aware that I was in the company of a man who had been tested to the extreme in his life, and who had experienced—beyond a shadow of a doubt—the unfailing trustworthiness of the living God. Again and again, he saw that what had been threatening him, or others, in the natural was dissolved by a greater, invisible power, and goodness had emerged.

As our relationship grew, both Neville and I increasingly saw this invisible power operating in melting bitterness between people and restoring relationships that had seemed broken beyond repair. We also both began to experience radical changes in our own hearts, and healings in our bodies that defied medical explanation. We witnessed transformation in others, too.

These profound experiences gave us the growing conviction that another Reality—another order of things—was much closer to us than our natural senses would indicate.

From then onwards, our mutual, fervent pursuit was to know Jesus Christ and to experience relationship with Him in ever-deeper measure. We longed to learn how to cooperate with Him in order to see the facts and the promises described in the Bible spring to life and make a difference on earth.

Neville described his relationship with Jesus as a "continuously flaming inner experience." He lived in an atmosphere of prayer and meditation, receiving revelation on Bible verses and different aspects of spiritual truth. He faithfully wrote them down and sought to put them into practice in his own life. He saw considerable fruit and was much encouraged along the way. At the same time, he remained humble and open.

He knew that these revelations and teachings were not just for his private consumption but for the benefit of present and future generations.

He has asked me to share them as widely as possible. To that end, this book contains the essence of his key teachings—and in some cases the teachings themselves, word for word—interspersed with aspects of Neville's biography that demonstrate the working of the Holy Spirit in his life.

I am also preparing a collection of Neville's written teachings for publication within the next few months, and some of his teachings are already accessible on his website, nevillejayaweera.com. It is helpful to know that many of the teachings on this website were written for people who had grown up within the Buddhist faith and were learning about Jesus Christ.

Neville's life was vibrant with prayer, writing, and helping others well into his late eighties. He went to heaven in May 2020 at the age of eighty-nine, but his love and his prophetic vision continue on in his writings and through the lives of the people he has helped and inspired.

The overarching aim of this book is to give glory to God, and to inspire readers by sharing the story—and the spiritual vision—of a most remarkable man who was utterly transformed by the love of God.

As I mention in the final chapter, one of the qualities that I valued most about Neville was that he demonstrated, and taught, how an intimate and dynamic relationship with God is accessible for everyone who chooses to pursue it.

Encounters—or meetings—with God can happen in countless ways. Some of them are visible or audible, but I think most are sensed as an impression in the heart or a gentle thought that flows in and enlightens the mind. They can be dramatic and unexpected but, equally, they can be quiet and almost imperceptible. Every experience with God is precious, and never to be underestimated.

It is clear in Scripture that God desires—and has made possible—an ongoing relationship of intimacy and Spirit-empowered living. This is His invitation to everyone, in every walk of life, and not just to spiritual giants and interstellar prophets!

No one is excluded. Everyone is invited to step into the radiant new life that has already been provided for us in Christ!

CHAPTER 1

A LONGING THAT WILL NOT SUBSIDE

ON THE SURFACE, THERE WERE no signs in Neville Jayaweera's childhood of the extraordinary spiritual experience that was to completely reframe his life. There was even less evidence of the formidable intellect and vision that would compel heads of state to seek his wisdom and counsel.

In fact, one of Neville's earliest schoolboy memories was an uncomfortable evening visit from his teacher, Ira, in 1936. She wanted the best for him, and expressed her concern that he was rather sloppy and untidy at school, and that his test results were keeping him at the bottom of the class. Well, second from bottom, to be precise.

That evening, Ira reluctantly told his mother that unless six-year-old Neville improved, and learned to add and subtract, he would not be promoted to the next class.

Happily, Neville's mother, Constance Jayaweera, was a serene bedrock of reassurance. His whole family was supportive, but his mother, in particular, had a strong sense that there was something very special about her son—despite his struggles at school—and she calmly encouraged him on, all throughout those early years.

She would often sweep him up onto her lap and assure him that everything would be absolutely fine. Little Neville found much solace and an unfailing source of strength as he nestled within the ample folds of her long sari.

The Jayaweera household was lively, to say the least. Neville was the third-born child, following his older brother, Stanley, and sister, Sheila. Then baby Beryl arrived to complete the quartet.

Neville's father was Robert Francis Jayaweera—well known and respected in the local community as a postmaster. His passion for discipline, hard work, and loyalty of service to Ceylon (renamed Sri Lanka in 1972) later became a marked driving force within Neville's own working life.

The family were practicing Buddhists, attending the local temple regularly, and they took seriously the Buddha's teachings on loving-kindness, generosity, forgiveness, and gentleness as a way of life.

Their house was set in a peaceful garden in Mount Lavinia, an ocean-lapped suburb on the outskirts of the capital city, Colombo. The breathtaking splendor of the ocean, with its miles of pristine, white sands, played a very important part in Neville's boyhood years, when he had grown old enough to go out by himself.

Instead of accepting invitations to play with his friends, he used to slip away quietly to gaze at the glory of the early evening stars and listen to the majestic roar of the ocean, which stretched from horizon to horizon.

He would listen intently to the alternating rhythm of cresting, crashing waves and gently whispering surf, mesmerized by the vastness and the sheer beauty that surrounded him on every side.

In the midst of it all, however, a mysterious feeling—like an intense longing—would increasingly pull and ache within his heart. As he gazed up at the glory of the star-laden sky night after night, tears would stream down his young cheeks.

But he did not know why.

Sometimes, on these walks, he would start to sing. But his mind did not really engage with what he was singing. Whatever was happening was all at the level of his heart.

One of the songs that poured out from within Neville, without him being aware of its significance, was the Christian hymn entitled "Abide with Me."

This may seem strange when his entire upbringing had been devoted to Buddhism. And it still was, within the family home, but the Christian influence came from a new school that he had entered for his secondary education.

With the support of his parents and his loyal teacher, Ira, Neville had managed to improve his grades and to make good progress at his primary school. So much so that he had gained a place at the well-regarded St. Thomas' College[1], near his home in Mount Lavinia. The school had been established by the Anglican Church and gained a reputation among the Buddhist community for its high standards of education and morals.

Part of his duties at St. Thomas' College was to attend services and to sing English hymns and carols. At a conscious level, the Christian content held no particular meaning for Neville, and he remained focused on his Buddhist practice. But clearly some of the words and music of "Abide with Me" had worked their way gently into his heart.

By contrast, the effects of other Christian compositions were a lot less subtle, and provoked chuckles and much humor among Neville and his classmates. For example, they simply could not see the relevance of singing "in the bleak midwinter," with its reference to snow falling upon snow, when they were all mopping their brows in the intense tropical heat of Ceylon!

Despite the cultural incongruities, Neville thrived throughout his senior school years. He read avidly, loved his studies, and discovered that he was well on track to pursue a law degree in Colombo.

Compared with the excitement of this new phase of life, the intense experience of his beach walks had become a rather veiled memory. But the experience had by no means disappeared altogether.

In fact, Neville's profound sense of longing surfaced once again in an extraordinary and totally unexpected way one afternoon, while he sat quietly in his parents' garden.

He suddenly fell into a trance-like state in which he had an open vision.

At that moment, everything seemed to dissolve around him. Plants, creatures, objects, the lawn—everything began to appear as pulsating, vibrating particles of light. He was at once caught up in an overwhelming sense of peace and completeness. It was an awesome and life-changing moment which he kept private, pondering upon it within his heart.

---

1   Subsequently renamed S. Thomas' College.

Change did not happen overnight, but that extraordinary moment caused Neville to reflect deeply upon what he had experienced. He probably could not put his finger on exactly when and where the change occurred, but it manifested a while later, while he was at university. To the consternation of his family, he changed course midstream to study philosophy instead of law.

This redirection reflected a major change in his mind and heart. He was turning away from the option of a lucrative career in law in favor of pursuing the unknown, for he was not sure what a degree in philosophy would bring. But he knew, without a doubt, that it would provide him with the opportunity to immerse himself in studying the fundamental nature of knowledge, reality, and existence.

He grasped the opportunity with enthusiasm and enjoyed his studies, as far as they went. But they did not really address the mysterious longings in his heart.

On graduation, in 1953, Neville accepted an invitation to remain at the university to teach aspects of philosophy, which he did for two years. Then, in 1955, his life took a very different turn when he joined the Ceylon Civil Service (CCS).

A strong driving force behind his application to join the Civil Service was Neville's desire to serve his country and all its people. In particular, he wanted to be able to impact the lives of the many who dwelled in impoverished and badly served rural areas.

To understand the power and authority attached to the organization he was about to join, it is helpful to know that, despite its name, the Ceylon Civil Service excluded most public servants. While Ceylon had over 200,000 government employees, the CCS itself comprised a small group numbering no more than 120. They were recruited directly from universities and then required to pass a notoriously stiff competitive exam before they could even begin their training.

In 1958, after his initial years of training with the CCS, Neville married Trixie Jayasekera, whom he had met at university, where she was studying for a general arts degree. Trixie soon proved to be the vital anchor of his home, holding steady when the surging seas of his career may well have toppled a less devoted craft.

Sea-surge number one came the following year when, at just twenty-nine years of age, Neville was appointed General Manager of a huge, multipurpose development project with 16,000 employees on the payroll. The project, called the Gal Oya Development Board (GODB), was organized around a dam and reservoir network that had been constructed across the Gal Oya river in Ceylon's Eastern Province.

At that time, the GODB was considered the most difficult managerial position under government because of its highly unionized and inflexible labor force. True to its reputation, the 16,000-strong workforce quickly and strategically ganged up on Neville to make it clear that *they* were the ones in control.

But Neville was undaunted. He knew the answer was to negotiate well and to be "hands on" as well as a firm manager. So he pulled up his sleeves and immersed himself into learning the elements of engineering and construction—no small task for a philosophy graduate.

Remarkably, within four intensive weeks, he had already established his authority, and he remained in managerial control for the following three years. When his assignment was completed, in 1963, the project was running as a sustainable enterprise for the first time in its twelve-year existence.

Ethnic Conflict and the Pursuit of Peace

If the job in Gal Oya was challenging, the position of government agent (administrative head) of the District of Jaffna was more daunting still. Even the most experienced civil servants avoided it like the plague because of its complex political situation and acute unrest.

In July 1963, the then prime minister of Ceylon, Mrs. Sirima Ratwatte Dias Bandaranaike, took the unusual step of personally visiting the Jayaweera family in their home. She appealed to Neville to take on the job of running Jaffna for the sake of the country.

Neville and Trixie felt they could not turn down her personal request, so they made their move to the northernmost tip of Ceylon and settled in Jaffna for the next three years.

This move reflected an aspect of Neville's career which was particularly close to his heart: peacemaking work that addressed Sri Lanka's ethnic conflict. The conflict was between the majority Sinhalese and the minority Tamils. Neville himself was Sinhala, but he hated discrimination and injustice of any kind.

The main problem in Jaffna, the capital of the Tamil people, was the refusal of the Tamils, who at that time comprised about 20 percent of the country's population, to accept what they saw as second-class citizenship and to live under the oppression of the Sinhala majority community.

Back in 1956, a strong Sinhala-dominated nationalist government had made the Sinhala language the only official language of the country. Tamils felt that they were being squeezed out of the educational system and public services, as well as losing their rights to retain their traditional lands.

Since 1956, the relationship between the Sinhala and Tamil communities had grown increasingly toxic, and the District of Jaffna had become virtually ungovernable.

Upon taking office in 1963, Neville soon found that the people of Jaffna had genuine grievances, and he was torn between his loyalty to government and his conscience. He chose the daunting option of seeing the prime minister, personally, and telling her that the policy of repression of the Tamils and confrontation with them would not prove of any benefit either to the Tamil people, or to the government, or to the country.

He respectfully said to her that if she still wanted him to continue as government agent of Jaffna, he would reverse the current policy of confrontation and repression hitherto adopted by the government and instead pursue a policy of consultation, mediation, and compromise.

Although initially shocked by Neville's audaciousness, Mrs. Bandaranaike relented—with the proviso that it was only a special dispensation granted to him for his administration of Jaffna. It was not to be understood as a change in national policy.

This was a most unusual outcome, to say the least. It meant, for example, that Neville could allow the Sinhala-only policy to lapse in Jaffna and introduce Tamil as a legally recognized language.

It took some months to convince Tamil leaders that this was not simply a passing tactic to take the heat off the issue. For Neville, the entire undertaking involved a lot of stress and certainly risk to his career and personal reputation. But the results were very rewarding for him—and for many in Jaffna.

However, even in the midst of such intense times of concentration and diplomacy, Neville was aware of living with a deep sense of contradiction.

He wrote of his time in Jaffna:

> I . . . confess that throughout my career . . . this contradiction has haunted me. While the great "Other", or the spiritual reality, kept stalking my mundane preoccupations . . .
>
> That is not to say that I refused to meet the world's demands upon my career, but that while fulfilling them with utmost intensity, I felt constantly overshadowed by a sense of unreality of what I was doing.
>
> The world saw only the mask, the disciplined and overbearing administrator who produced results regardless, but it had no sense of the inner torment that the mask concealed.[2]

He longed to be free from the underlying sense of meaninglessness, but its suffocating bonds pursued Neville increasingly during the first four decades of his life. He didn't know what Reality looked like, or felt like, but deep within his being, he knew that there was something more to life than met the eye or the ear, or human logic. But he didn't know how to find it, and he felt very alone.

---

2   Neville Jayaweera, *Jaffna: Exorcising the Past and Holding the Vision. An Autobiographical Reflection on the Ethnic Conflict* (Colombo: Ravaya Publishers, 2014). Out of print.

Even then, he wasn't truly alone. Some years later, after his spiritual awakening in 1970, Neville said he could see how the Holy Spirit had been guiding him during his peacemaking efforts in Jaffna. By pursuing principles of justice and fair play, Neville succeeded in establishing goodwill between the government and the Tamil people, and during the three years he held this post, there was peace and harmony throughout the district. That was remarkable, given the deep-rooted history of conflict.

The first fruits of Neville's endeavors to bring about a reconciliation between the majority Sinhala community and the minority Tamil community became visible when, within two years of his taking on the job of Jaffna's government agent, a new government was formed including the Tamil parties.

Overcoming the antipathy that had separated the Sinhala and the Tamil people for hundreds of years, and being able to grant to the Jaffna District an administration that was free from tension and conflict, even for the three years he was administrative head, gave Neville great satisfaction.

However, within a year of his departure from Jaffna, the government in Colombo squandered all the gains he had made during his three-year tour there. The subsequent resumption of hostilities caused Neville deep distress, and he felt acutely that the government failed to grasp opportunities to prevent the escalation of war. The Sinhala-Tamil coalition broke apart, and the conflict raised its ugly head again, building up to the country's civil war (1983–2009) with its unspeakable misery and terrible loss of life.

Limitations and Regrets

In the twenty-eight years between his work in Jaffna and his ambassadorial post relating to the same issue, Neville wrote articles on the ethnic conflict for Sri Lanka's national press, and he was frequently called upon for his insights and advice. He remained, nevertheless, acutely conscious of the limitations of peacemaking initiatives, as well as the shortcomings of development work—such as the Gal Oya project. Neville had wanted to do so much more to resource and empower the marginalized sectors of Sri Lankan society.

Later, he also became painfully aware of his own, personal failings that blighted his high-flying career assignments. He wondered to what degree the indulgence of his ego had fueled his passionate commitment to work for the good of the country and its people. He wasn't sure which of these two sets of motivations was uppermost, but realized that they were very closely entwined.

The sharp recollection of his arrogance and the dominant quality of his personality caused Neville deep regret and remorse. He had an immense confidence in his ability to perform whatever assignment he was given. This had been fostered by the fact that successive governments had cherry-picked him for high-profile assignments that were far above his seniority in the Service.

He was driven by an almost fanatical commitment to discipline, punctuality, and integrity in public life. He said public servants must be prepared to make sacrifices and not think in terms of the regulation eight-hour working day or nursing their holidays and perks.

He used to tell his senior staff that if they wanted to be effective leaders, they must set an example by working twice or even three times as hard as their subordinates. These qualities and values, which Neville demonstrated in his own working life, garnered admiration and respect, but he was seen as intolerant and lacking compassion.

Looking back on his time with the Gal Oya development project, he reflected that although he had huge success in terms of the impression he made on political bosses and employees, he also committed many errors in its management.

As he said in his memoirs of the time, he was too young and inexperienced to appreciate the enormity of the task, and had looked on it primarily as an opportunity to enforce his personality and will.

When he left his Jaffna post in 1966, Neville had all the reasons in the world to believe his intellect and will could accomplish anything—except, perhaps, find the answers to his spiritual questions. The more deeply he searched for meaning, the more entrapped and dissatisfied with life he felt, despite his outer achievements.

His pursuit was twofold in purpose. One part of it was to understand and to escape from the mysterious pain that he felt in his heart. The other was to actively pursue the evidence he had received that there was another, indescribably attractive world—or *something*—that can be experienced beyond the reach of the five senses.

This map shows Neville's birthplace and home, Colombo, and the two other locations that also played an important role in his life—Jaffna and Vavuniya. (Ceylon was renamed Sri Lanka in 1972.)

CHAPTER 2

A LUMINOUS ENCOUNTER

BEFORE WE DIVE INTO NEVILLE'S next, weighty government assignment—and into all that lies beyond it—I would like to share a few insights into some of the other, more private, aspects of his character at the time.

In the workplace, people mainly saw Neville's formidable intellect and razor-sharp mind, which could rapidly penetrate the thickest of political problems and emerge with a viable answer. He radiated a sense of invincible authority.

However, in his personal life, he was private and somewhat shy, never wanting the limelight—although that was difficult to avoid. His older brother, Stanley, and friends would tease him lovingly: "What *is* it about you, Neville?! You are short and squat and balding . . . and yet you have a constant stream of admirers!"

The irony was that Neville never sought "admirers," let alone a constant stream of them. He shied away from such attention whenever he could, but his personality still attracted people to him. Part of the attraction was an exceptional gift of communication. You could hear a pin drop when he spoke, so magnetic and compelling were his words.

In public, Neville came across as a very serious person, speaking only about things and events that affected his work and the national interest. But those who knew him saw the much larger picture of a thoughtful and gentle man who was devoted to his family, faithful to his friends, and discreetly active in support of neighbors who needed help.

Perhaps one of his most noted characteristics was his ebullient sense of humor. Gales of laughter emerging from the homes of family and friends were a sure indication that Neville was among their company. He had a wonderful wit and a fine sense of the absurd, being very ready to tell stories against himself. His anecdotes would keep them in stitches, and caused many a tummy to ache with laughter.

He remained very close to both his parents, who passed down to him their standards of absolute integrity, among many other qualities. He followed the traditional greeting of touching their feet, especially if he had not seen them for some time; not in an attitude of worship but in tender affection and respect. Neville also dearly loved his sisters, Beryl and Sheila, and recalled the blessings of a peaceful and disciplined home life together with them and his brother, Stanley.

Another strong influence on Neville, as we saw earlier, was his local Buddhist temple, where he had learned most of the soft virtues that defined his character, such as kindness, honesty, equanimity, and the abhorrence of taking life in any form.

I remember him telling me about an extreme jolt of revulsion that he experienced when he moved a stone in his parents' garden and uncovered a large scorpion devouring some hapless, still-living creature—crunch by crunch, and bit by bit. This kind of scene would not have been new to Neville, of course. But, at that particular moment, it represented much more than a common scene in a garden. It was like a metaphor for a universal disorder that he could perceive but could not articulate. It left him feeling acutely distressed, with an almost unbearable surge of longing for a different world.

This was a touch of the Holy Spirit—similar to the touch he had received on his beach walks as a young boy. Deep within his heart, things continued to stir that he could not understand. They would bubble to the surface on rare occasions—such as this one, prompted by the scorpion—but then they would become veiled once more beneath the intense demands of his career.

Political Rumblings

Given Neville's proven gift as a communicator, perhaps it is not surprising that his next government appointment was very much to do with communication. He was asked to step into the role of chairman and director general of the Ceylon Broadcasting Corporation, which he ful-filled from 1966 to 1970.

It might have sounded like a peaceful oasis, after the challenges of Jaffna, but in fact the Corporation was in disarray and riddled with politi-cal interference. It was anything but peaceful. As a result, previous direc-tor generals had come and gone like yo-yos, unable to cope. There had been eleven in eight years.

One of the first things Neville did was ask that there should be no interference in decisions on programming or news, or in anything at all to do with administration. The minister who appointed him, Mr. Junius Richard Jayewardene, was taken aback by Neville's audacity, but never-theless, he consented to this request.

Neville transformed the Broadcasting Corporation during his four-year tenure. He was held in high regard and trust by the then prime minis-ter, Dudley Senanayake, who asked him to undertake special assignments for the government that went beyond Neville's remit in broadcasting.

At the Corporation, Neville framed a new broadcasting policy and harnessed some programming in line with government aims to advance development and benefit society, including a national initiative to make the country self-sufficient in food. He coped with politically motivated trade unions, restored a culture of discipline and integrity among the three thousand employees, and insulated the Corporation from political interference.

It is easy to sum up these achievements in a couple of sentences, but—not surprisingly—the environment in which they were gained was not always as straightforward. Some powerful political elements and trade union leaders were less than happy at the outcome.

In fact, by 1970, they were fuming—and they would soon have an oppor-tunity to express their vitriol, alongside others displeased with Ceylon's political landscape. In that year's parliamentary election, there was another electoral swing: Mr. Senanayake, with his center-right United National Party, was voted out, and Mrs. Bandaranaike, with the democratic socialist Sri Lanka Freedom Party, returned for her second term as prime minister.

Neville was undeterred by this political change because he believed in serving the nation rather than any particular party; he held strongly to the principle that, as a civil servant, he was called to be politically impartial and to serve the government of the day to the very best of his ability. He had already served under three changes of government and was held in high regard by the respective prime ministers. He had no reason to believe that it would be any different this time. It was, therefore, with a relatively routine and calm state of mind that Neville closed his office door at the Ceylon Broadcasting Corporation at the end of his assignment, and bid farewell to his colleagues.

Certainly, he anticipated that the forthcoming change of government would bring with it the shake-up and reshuffling of roles that usually accompany a new regime. To Neville, such change was simply an expected part of normal political procedure. However, what actually unfolded went way beyond a normal shake-up. Events swiftly began to unravel in a shocking way, particularly for Neville.

Out of the blue, he suddenly found himself subjected to a vicious assault upon his reputation and character by members of the new government. In no time at all, politically motivated venom, including lies about his behavior in office and allegations of corruption (all of which were subsequently officially investigated and proved false), were spreading like wildfire through the news media all over the island.

It came as no surprise to Neville that a new governing party would want to make changes in key leadership positions. That he could understand. But what he could *not* comprehend was the degree of hate that was leveled against him, when he was just trying to do his job to the best of his ability.

The mass media took delight in fanning the flames of vitriol. Worse still, a number of colleagues whom Neville trusted and respected had begun to raise their voices against him. Prominent among them were former coworkers who were now members of Mrs. Bandaranaike's newly elected government.

Allegedly, colleagues were accusing Neville of disloyalty. Some considered it a deep offense that he would serve the government of Prime Minister Dudley Senanayake with the same degree of attentiveness with which he had served Mrs. Bandaranaike's previous administration.

On top if it all, Neville abruptly received notice that the new government had assigned him to the role of administrative head (his official title being Government Agent) of a northern jungle outpost called Vavuniya, which lay so low in the national pecking order that it did not have even one solitary member of parliament to represent its interests.

This assignment was clearly designed to humiliate Neville. Vavuniya was well known to be a place where officials who had fallen out of favor with the government were sidelined for years on end, deprived of the comforts of home and family.

Surely, there had been a huge mistake. He was left reeling—to say the least. He knew not what to do, except to honor his Civil Service pledge to serve wherever his government asked him to go.

In May 1970, he packed his bags, bid a heartfelt farewell to his wife and baby daughter—he felt it was safest for them to remain in their Colombo home—and made the long journey to the jungles of Vavuniya.

Despite the negative reasons for his move to Vavuniya, Neville could appreciate the positive aspects of his new environment. He loved nature and the rich wildlife of the jungle. Above all, he felt deeply for the hard lives of the scattered groups of villagers, and wanted to serve them in the very best way that he could.

He wrote in his diary: "The mass of the people are very poor, living by cultivating paddy and cash crops which they sell to middlemen at ridiculously low prices. One of my multifarious tasks is to organize the marketing of the villagers' produce through government channels which guarantee them earnings above the market price."

More than 70 percent of the district was covered under a thick jungle canopy, where herds of elephants, leopards, bear, deer, and wild boar roamed unmolested—any shooting for "sport" being prohibited by law.

The entire district of about 150,000 people was served by a single hospital with just fifty beds. The small town of Vavuniya had one straggling high street with various shops and businesses, Buddhist and Hindu temples, an Anglican church, and a police station.

Neville was the government agent of the whole area, but the district was also served by a team of government officials, each representing a government department in the capital, Colombo.

So Neville wasn't alone physically, but emotionally and spiritually he felt very alone indeed. There was absolutely no one with whom he could share his inner turmoil—and he would not know what to say, anyway.

His residence in Vavuniya—built originally as the residency for British officers during the colonial era—only served to emphasize his isolation. It was an enormous mansion which, he observed, "stood out like a sore thumb in contrast with the dwellings of the local villagers who eked out a precarious living in their wattle and daub huts."

Every day, he served the local population the best he could. Then, when his small staff left for the day and the long, solitary evening stretched ahead of him, he tried desperately to make sense of what had happened. But he could not.

Blatant lies and accusations had rained down on him like burning acid. He couldn't escape them, even in the jungle. Neville's friends and colleagues had urged him fervently to speak up, but he did not retaliate even once or try to defend himself through the media. He could very easily have done so. Instead, he absorbed it all upon his mind and heart.

He pored over events in his memory—well aware that he had never been everyone's "cup of tea." That tends to go with the territory if you are in a senior management role, and a governmental one at that. From the time he was twenty-nine, Neville's career path had soared upwards like a meteor, in an unprecedented way in the country. He had gained a reputation as a very strong and productive leader and had been appointed to influential positions irrespective of the political party that happened to be in power—until this latest government shift.

Neville recognized that his meteoric achievements had come at some cost to his relationships. As he reflected, he could see the costs to his character as well. But he knew that integrity and morality had remained vital to him, and he couldn't think of any time he'd compromised those values in public or in private. He had always been rigorously honest and fair in his dealings, and he went to extremes to ensure transparency in all his activities.

So to be accused of a whole host of wrongdoings . . . and by people who knew him . . . it was just too much to bear.

He felt completely broken. For all his adult life, his keen intellect and ability to see right through to the heart of things had served him exceptionally well. But they were of no use to him now. Nothing made sense. Everything he relied on seemed to have disintegrated around him and within him.

The only thing he could be sure of was the searing pain in his mind and heart. He had to do *something*, but really, he didn't know what to do.

Night after night, he sat alone in his incongruously grand mansion and immersed himself in every philosophical and meditative discipline he could think of. He was straining for answers.

He first applied himself to two of the profound and rigorous meditative disciplines at the heart of Buddhist teaching: Maitri Bhavana meditation, which is a meditation on extending loving-kindness to everyone, without exception; and Vipassana Bhavana meditation, which seeks insight and clear awareness of exactly what is happening as it happens.

I recall him telling me later that he would alter his normal routines in an attempt to make the meditations more effective. Anything in order to bring some shaft of light into his situation. So, for example, if he felt inclined to rest, he would do the opposite, and force himself to get up and move around. He would rigorously discipline his mind and his body.

Neville also applied himself intensely to the Hindu Advaita meditative discipline, including the Neti-Neti meditation (the truth is "neither this nor that") as taught by two of India's greatest Hindu philosophers and sages, Adi Shankara (700 AD) and Ramana Maharshi (1900 AD).

Those disciplines, profound though they were, failed to provide him with the answers he was seeking.

A Luminous Encounter

Then one night, while Neville was sitting in meditation, something utterly extraordinary and totally unexpected happened. He suddenly found himself swept up in an awesome, luminous experience that was sacred and altogether "Other." He was overwhelmed beyond measure.

Waves of Love swept in like a flood, penetrating every fiber of his mind, his heart, and his body. It was as though he was, literally, being refashioned and being made completely new from the inside out. This sense of newness transcended anything he had ever known before. No words could come near to describing it. He intuitively knew it was Jesus Christ, but that was the extent of his comprehension.

The experience was indeed wondrous, and all the more so because he had not been seeking Jesus at all! In fact, he had never felt drawn to Christianity; his search had focused solely on the Buddhist and Hindu traditions with which he had grown up and which were an integral and very important part of his life.

Not surprisingly, his mind began swirling with questions, but it was Neville's heart, not his mind, that led the way now—with answers bubbling up that far surpassed any human explanation. His heart was being radically and irreversibly melted. It was as though a thousand suns were beaming down upon a dense, deep arctic iceberg. The ice was powerless to do anything but to yield to the searing heat, and its waters—imprisoned for long years—began to flow and leap and dance in the brilliant light.

In Neville's own words: "As I looked out of my upstairs bedroom window even the trees and the foliage seemed to be doing a dance."

The atmosphere was suffused with light, joy, and peace. Even the purple-faced leaf monkeys, who would raid Neville's mango tree and then quickly scamper away, changed their behavior and just sat there, gazing at him. Normally, at Neville's approach, the monkeys would scatter through the branches in all directions, grasping the purloined fruits against their chests. But on this occasion they stayed close to him, and even stretched out their arms to offer him some of the mangoes they had stolen! It was as though Neville had entered into another world.

In the days that followed, his daily schedule remained pretty much the same. He still got up as normal in the morning, greeted his staff, assigned

their duties, and continued his appointed work as the government agent
of the District of Vavuniya.

Outwardly things were the same, but inwardly they were very different
indeed. Now, Neville saw his work, his life—indeed everything—through
completely different eyes. He wrote in his diary:

> Following that experience I felt as light as a feather, as if gravity
> itself could no longer hold me and as if I was levitating far above
> the earth.
>
> Love and forgiveness towards all beings, friend and foe
> alike, most of all towards those who had abused me, and indeed
> towards all creation, streamed out from me and spilled over
> into my environment.
>
> My staff, who had generally cowered in my presence, now
> approached me with broad smiles as if to say, "You have changed,
> Sir! What has happened?"—as if the tsunami of Love had washed
> over them as well!

One of the first things that Neville did in the wake of this luminous
experience was to write and apologize to all his employees and aides whom
he had disciplined or treated harshly over the years, asking them to forgive
him. They were deeply touched and amazed by the transformation in this
man, whom they had known as an arrogant bureaucrat who was authori-
tarian, intolerant, and harsh. Neville's letters of apology and requests for
forgiveness were also extended to those colleagues who had slandered and
wrongly accused him. They, too, were astonished by this radical change—
and totally perplexed!

※

ENCOUNTER—AN INVITATION FOR EVERYONE

The outpouring of love and peace that flooded Neville when he encountered Jesus Christ completely transformed his life from that moment onwards.
The shards of ice that had long been stabbing at his heart—shards of pain,

confusion, bitterness, emptiness—all melted in an instant. To his amazement, love had suddenly become his all-consuming reason for existence.

Neville's encounter with God was indeed extraordinary. But isn't it true that every single encounter with the Creator of the universe is extraordinary? Whether it occurs in a dramatic way or in a much quieter, almost imperceptible way—such as a gentle impression on the heart—each encounter is equally holy and precious.

What does it mean to encounter God? The word "encounter" means to meet personally. It carries the sense of an individual experience of God and can take many different forms. It can be a physical encounter, a stirring of the heart, a revelation or a picture in the mind, a pricking of the conscience, or a deep sense of reverence—to name but a few examples. For myself, encounters are gentle and, in the past, I think I have probably dismissed many as "just a feeling" or "just my imagination." But I'm learning to take more heed now.

Have you ever had the experience of reading a passage of Scripture and suddenly seeing it in a new way? A sort of "Oh, I see!" moment? Well, the Word of God is "alive and active" (Heb. 4:12) . . . and in that moment you had an encounter with Jesus, the living Word! The mark of a genuine encounter is that it fosters goodness—the fruit of the Holy Spirit.

Neville's extraordinary encounter with God may be very different from your own experience of God, and mine. It's tempting to think that his remarkable story doesn't actually relate to our lives in a tangible, significant way. But it *does* relate to us—very much so. It is a reminder that God's desire is to meet with each of us personally.

Encounter with God Is an Ongoing Experience

An encounter with God is not a one-off experience. Each one is an invitation to enter ever more deeply into relationship with the Creator of the universe. In other words, to enter into an ongoing, eternal encounter with the One who loves us with a burning, unending love.

The word "encounter" is a helpful expression to describe our awakening to a very wonderful truth: that in fact there is no longer any distance between us and God. All separation was abolished at the cross. The staggering truth of the Gospel is that we are now united with God. The issue is our conscious awareness of—and sensitivity to—this mind-bending fact.

Whether we "feel" it or not, the death and resurrection of Jesus Christ has already brought every single one of us into complete union with God. We are already "face-to-face" with Him—He indwells us and occupies the most intimate of relationships with us. Our role is, progressively, to awaken to this truth, and the experiences that we call encounters are all part of the process of awakening.

Let's look at some scriptural examples of people's encounters with God—all very different.

The apostle Paul had, perhaps, one of the most dramatic encounters recorded in the New Testament. On the road to Damascus, Paul was blinded by a light from heaven, and he heard the voice of Jesus asking him, "Why are you persecuting Me?" (Acts 9:4). The result of that experience was massive transformation in Paul's life. This man, who had zealously persecuted Christians, became their greatest supporter and a fervent devotee of Jesus Christ.

Paul had other dramatic encounters, too, such as when he was "caught up into Paradise and heard inexpressible words" (2 Cor. 12:4), and when he and Silas were worshipping while in prison, and an earthquake broke open the prison doors and loosed their chains (Acts 16:23–26).

I think it is deeply significant that Paul was not distracted by these and the many other dramatic happenings that he experienced from the Lord. He valued them, certainly, as is evident in his writing and reports, but he didn't get stuck on them. They were simply springboards to take him deeper and deeper into his one all-consuming passion: the Lord Jesus. His heartfelt cry remained humble and laser-focused right up to his final imprisonment in Rome: "that I may know Him [Jesus Christ]" (Phil. 3:10).

Encounter through Inner Revelation

An example of encounter with God in the gospel accounts includes the remarkable experience of Bartimaeus, who was a blind beggar. This was the man who came face to face with the Son of God and heard the words

"Go your way; your faith has made you well" (Mark 10:52). That is remark-able enough, but perhaps it is just as remarkable that even before he stood in front of the Word made flesh, Bartimaeus had—inwardly—already "met" with the Living Word. We know he had received a revelation that Jesus was the Son of David, the promised Messiah, because he cried "Son of David, have mercy on me!" (Mark 10:49). That was the fruit of an inner, invisible, but very real encounter. And it came to someone whom society would have categorized as a most unlikely kind of person to receive favor from God.

Yet another form of encounter appears in the book of Acts when an angel of the Lord spoke to Philip, saying, "Arise and go toward the south along the road which goes down from Jerusalem to Gaza" (Acts 8:26). As Philip journeyed, the Spirit then spoke, guiding him to a chariot carrying a high-ranking eunuch who was returning to Ethiopia. The man was reading verses from Isaiah 53, which he could not understand, and he invited Philip to sit in his chariot and explain them. It was an amazing, God-inspired meeting . . . in the middle of a desert! The eunuch certainly had his own personal encounter with God that day, declaring his conviction that Jesus Christ is indeed the Son of God, and receiving baptism from Philip.

As you read Neville's life story and experiences in the pages of this book, I encourage you to engage with the occasions and words that inspire you. Even though Neville's context may vary greatly from your own, God transcends culture and time and can speak to our individual hearts to bring us into an ever-greater awareness of His Person and Presence. "Jesus Christ is the same yesterday, today, and forever" (Heb. 13:8), and what He does in the life of one human being—in this case, Neville—He can do in the lives of others in ways that speak directly and uniquely to each person.

CHAPTER 3

PEACE IN THE MIDST OF TURMOIL

FOR NEVILLE, IT STARTED WITH reports of unusual activities in his area: groups of young people were holding secret meetings in the jungle; they were seen wearing strange blue uniforms; guns were vanishing from village homes. Similar reports were reaching Colombo from districts all across the island. By early March 1971, it was clear to everyone that the country was on the threshold of a major uprising.[3]

An organized group calling themselves the JVP was about to launch a nationwide attempt to overthrow the government and establish a Marxist state. The JVP, which stands for Janatha Vimukthi Peramuna—The People's Liberation Front—was largely made up of some fifty thousand young people from the Sinhalese—the largest ethnic group on the island.

The uprising was not caused by ethnic differences, as happened in later years. Rather, it was a class struggle—an attempt by marginalized people, who constantly felt oppressed and invisible in society, to gain a share in state power. Their cause was just but, tragically, their means were violent.

---

3   Sources: The accounts of events in Vavuniya are drawn from Neville's personal diaries and from his book *The Vavuniya Diaries* (Colombo: Ravaya Publishers, 2017) (out of print). I have narrated the accounts in my own words while basing the text closely on Neville's writings, and citing his direct quotations where appropriate.

The planned strategy of the JVP activists was to coordinate a simultaneous attack on all police stations throughout the country, seize their arms, and train them on the government. An essential part of their strategy was to capture and assassinate all government agents and senior government officials, which would enable the JVP to cripple the national administration.

As government agent of Vavuniya, Neville was well aware that he was a prime and juicy target for the JVP.

An observer could say that it looked as though Neville had been completely stitched up and hung out to dry. Even when he was appointed, back in May the previous year, his government knew conflict was brewing and that Vavuniya's government agent would need military knowledge and expertise to execute his responsibilities. And his government knew Neville had no such expertise.

They assigned him anyway. The situation looked very bleak. Neville and his colleagues were indeed facing a life-and-death situation. They had no option but to prepare for the worst.

The government responded to the growing crisis by stepping up their military and police reinforcements to all "critical areas," but it quickly became apparent that Vavuniya was not considered a critical area. They ignored Neville's pleas for military reinforcements, and he felt, increasingly, that in the government's eyes he was a non-person, a sacrificial lamb.

The one comfort he had, after his encounter with the Sacrificial Lamb just a few months earlier, was that he could rely on the Lord's presence.

As March wore on, the only additional support that turned up was some two-way high-frequency radio equipment. Neville was grateful, even for this most modest of provisions! Neville kept supplying the Colombo command center (based at the prime minister's official residence) with daily reports on the deepening crisis in his district. However, he received no feedback at all, and his repeated requests for a platoon of infantry went unheeded.

So he decided he would forage for some military help on his own. He knew there were some infantry platoons stationed just fifty-five miles away, in Mannar, where they were not likely to be needed. They were under the command of Lt. Colonel Denis[4] Hapugalle, a personal friend whom he felt free to approach. On the evening of 4 April, he asked Samson, his chauffeur, to drive him to Mannar to meet with Denis at his residency.

In conversation over dinner together, Denis expressed great sympathy for Neville's predicament, but he couldn't grant his friend's request for more soldiers. Denis explained that he himself was out of favor with the Colombo command center, adding that he was unlikely to receive permission to move his troops to Vavuniya. Without that permission, Denis would be violating military law.

They had finished dinner and were into coffee when a police jeep roared down the driveway and screeched to a halt outside Denis's residency. A greatly agitated police sergeant jumped out and ran to tell Neville that the police inspector of Vavuniya, Richard Udugampola, was looking frantically for him. He said that a number of police stations in his district were already under attack, and an attack on Vavuniya itself was imminent.

Moral and Spiritual Tumult

At Neville's direction, Samson raced back through the dense Parayanalankulam jungle, leaving bewildered on the roadside man, wild buffalo, and rogue elephant alike, covering some fifty-five miles in barely thirty-five minutes. They reached home shortly before midnight. At his residency, Neville listened to the heavy radio traffic jamming the air waves. Police station after police station was reporting concerted attacks. Some stations had already been overrun by the rebels.

A crunch of boots outside the building announced Richard Udugampola, the inspector of the Vavuniya police station, as he rushed inside to give Neville the news: Two neighboring police stations were under attack. The inspector expected an attack on his station at any moment, and he feared his men may not stand up and fight. What did Neville think he should do?

As Neville listened to the police inspector, he was painfully aware that even though he was responsible *overall* for law and order within it, he was

---

4   Also spelled Dennis

nevertheless only a civilian, with no responsibility whatsoever for actually taking charge of police stations.

Much less for bearing arms!

Besides, his own spiritual unfoldment of the previous few months had made him singularly unfit for the role that was being cast for him. The thought of killing anybody, even in self-defense or in the line of duty, made him tremble. But he knew he had to provide leadership.

Contradictory thoughts and impulses raced through Neville's mind as he thought of Trixie and their infant daughter, Mano, sleeping peacefully in her cot far down south in Colombo. The moral and spiritual tumult was tearing his insides apart. He felt as if clouds of butterflies had been let loose inside his stomach, and his knees were giving way. With supreme effort, Neville pulled himself together and addressed the inspector: "Please be seated and I shall join you in a few minutes."

So saying, he walked upstairs to his bedroom, fell to his knees, and wept.

Neville felt an overpowering dread. He was not afraid for his life. It was simply that he could not handle the contradiction between his spiritual commitment on one hand and his duty in the crisis, on the other. A year earlier, when he was a man of the world, confident in his ability to resolve seemingly impossible situations, he would have embraced the challenge to prove himself—even though he'd have abhorred the prospect of violence of any kind.

Now, however, his whole approach was completely different: he felt so uncertain . . . so broken . . . so weak.

However, as he knelt and prayed through his tears in the silence, he felt a strange metamorphosis taking place. It was as if he had tapped into a hidden reservoir of power and a life-giving fountain began to bubble up within him. Then, from the depths of the inner silence, a voice came to him with authority and power:

"Be glad you are nothing, and can be nothing. Let Me take over. Let Me be your strength and your wisdom. Have no malice towards anyone and consider no one your enemy.

"Just trust in Me and lean on Me and I shall be unto you all you need for the moment. I shall never leave you, never forsake you. You shall neither stumble, nor lack for courage or wisdom, for I go with you. Fear for nothing. Get up and go."

That was it. The veil of indecision and doubt had been lifted. An indescribable new energy surged through Neville. He picked up a shotgun from the residence and walked down the stairs, filled with a newfound resolve.

He knew with an unerring certainty what he had to do. Although he had a gun in his hand, he had neither hate nor fear in his heart, and he knew he was not going to kill or injure anyone. He just had a role to play and a duty to perform, and felt equal to both.

The police inspector stared in amazement at the unlikely vision of Neville, his civilian government agent, coming down the staircase with a shotgun, and even wearing a string of cartridges around his waist!

Very calmly, Neville said, "Let's go, Inspector."

The two men strode out into the cool night air to walk the two hundred yards to the police station, followed by Neville's faithful houseboy, Amarasiri, who insisted on bringing up the rear with nothing more lethal than a flask of hot coffee.

Encouraging Disgruntled Zombies

The time was shortly after midnight, the beginning of 5 April 1971—a day which is engraved in the annals of modern Sri Lanka.

When they reached the police station, Neville immediately saw that the men had no intention of following orders to fight.

In a trice, the real problem dawned on Neville. Most of these men had been unwillingly transferred to Vavuniya, and separated from their families, due to falling out of favor with government in some way—rather like Neville himself!

They were deeply disgruntled and saw no reason why they should risk their lives to defend a government which they felt had wronged them. No wonder the inspector had sought help.

Neville had to act fast. He asked the sergeant to get his men to "fall in" as if on parade. He explained to them how he himself happened to be in Vavuniya as the government agent, and how he felt as wronged as any of them. However, he said, they were all public servants, and the police have a duty to defend the government in power at all times, even if it meant risking their lives.

Lastly, he assured them that even though he was not in the police, and risking his life was not among his duties, he had decided to fight alongside them. In proof of that, Neville held his gun aloft so that all could see. "Sir," said one man, "if you talk like that, we are prepared to lay down our own lives."

Men who five minutes earlier were like zombies in slow motion suddenly switched to fast-forward. They laced up their boots, fastened their belts, unchained their rifles from the rack, filled their belt pouches with ammunition, and soon began to look as if they could take on the very forces of hell.

Within fifteen minutes, Neville and the police inspector had thirty men under arms, serving alongside them in appointed positions. They turned off the lights and waited for the attack to come. The time was shortly after one in the morning.

An hour passed, but aside from an occasional snore from a policeman and the screeching of bats that went about their nocturnal business, nothing dramatic happened. Neville began to notice that the orchestra of snoring policemen was rising to a crescendo. Should the rebels draw close in the darkness, the snoring would give them an idea of their state of preparedness.

He had to do something to wake them up and keep them alert. He called for Samson and asked him to go in a police jeep to the all-night coffee shop on the high street and bring a bucket of hot coffee. Then he sent the word round that every alternate man should come for a coffee break to the jeep, ensuring that each position was still held by at least one man. Fifteen of the thirty men under arms quickly huddled round the jeep to have coffee.

The next thing they knew, shotgun pellets were raining down upon them. Three of Neville's group, including the sergeant, fell to the ground on the first volley. More than four of the men drinking coffee broke and ran, throwing down their rifles, and hid inside a barrel drain that ran in front of the station. Within thirty seconds, their strength had dwindled to just twenty men, and they had been alerted by informers to expect an assault by between one hundred and two hundred rebels. The situation looked hopeless.

However, the remnant of the Vavuniya police under Inspector Udugampola fought back with great valor. In the very first round of the firefight, the policemen hit the rebel leader, one Obeywansa, who was spearheading the assault. He had led his men to within a few yards of the building when he was hit and killed by a bullet from a police rifle. There was nothing Neville could do—he found it heartrending. But this JVP tragedy most probably saved the police station. When the leader fell, his men panicked, broke off the charge, and retreated in confusion. Badly demoralized, the rebels did not attempt a direct human wave assault thereafter. However, they were clever tacticians. They kept up a steady fusillade from hidden positions, provoking the Vavuniya police to shoot back wildly and thus expend ammunition rapidly.

After one hour it became clear to Neville that they could not hold out for long, and the rebels knew it, too. Then an idea flashed into his mind. He crawled on his knees to the telephone on the inspector's desk and was amazed to find that the rebels hadn't cut the telephone lines. He called the radio men working from the residency and dictated a signal to the command center in Colombo explaining the situation and making yet another appeal for reinforcements.

Completely Composed and at Peace

Even as Neville made this call, in the face of such extreme danger, he was completely composed and at peace within himself. He felt neither fear nor hatred towards anyone, and his reliance was neither in guns, nor in ammunition, nor in the promised reinforcements. Indeed, he felt no desire to overrun a supposed enemy but felt throughout a Presence and a Power whose strength far exceeded their human material resources.

He knew they would come through.

As he crouched at a window with his gun's safety catch off, he was able to reflect on the contradiction and the absurdity of it all. He later wrote about those reflections in his diary: "If I could disembody myself, I would hover over the scene completely untouched by what was happening below, seeing neither police nor rebel, neither friend nor foe, but just human ignorance, an illusion, masquerading as reality, with no more substance to it than a dream."

As Neville and the men waited, they observed that rebel fire had died down and the remaining rebels had retreated. Then they saw the eastern sky already tinged with the dawn: they had made it through the night. They were now able to see the casualties, including the body of the rebel leader lying on the sand. The police busied themselves attending to the wounded and dispatching men to the hospital.

Neville spoke to every one of the police constables who survived, and thanked them for their bravery and devotion to duty. Then he asked Samson to drive him back to the residency, where he could ready himself for the conflict ahead.

❧

VENTURING OUT WITH GOD

Neville's unusual circumstances served to propel him into a deep dive with God. He began to follow the promptings of the Spirit[5] before he was consciously aware that that was even possible; let alone that it was a biblical instruction! I think it would be true to say that most believers progress more gradually into their relationship with God. But the principles are the same.

It's worth noting here that Neville's spiritual life didn't *always* flow with such immediate intimacy and power. Over the years that followed, he had to exercise much patience, endure seasons of wilderness, and cling to the Truth revealed in God's Word when everything in the natural seemed to be screaming the opposite. Transitioning from our earthly "old-Adam"

---

5   See Romans 8:4, PHILLIPS.

life into the New Creation life offered to us in Christ is never a quick fix, but, as Neville would often say, it's the only way worth living and the most glorious path!

The threatening circumstances in Vavuniya that caused Neville to hurl himself entirely upon the mercy and wisdom of God actually served to transport him into the foundational truth of New Creation living. The apostle Paul expresses it this way: "My old identity has been co-crucified with Christ and no longer lives. And now the essence of this new life is no longer mine, for the Anointed One lives his life through me" (Gal. 2:20, TPT).

In those moments of utter weakness and anguish, Neville heard God speaking to him, and the words had an extraordinary and transcendent effect on Neville's entire being:

"Be glad you are nothing, and can be nothing. Let Me take over. Let Me be your strength and your wisdom." These words carried the enabling power of the Holy Spirit within them: the supernatural grace to surrender completely—in that moment. To surrender human thinking and logic; to lay them down and wait in faith for God's wisdom and empowerment. In doing so, Neville discovered that the Spirit did indeed flow into the vacuum to be the strength and wisdom that guided him through that critical day. He also learned, in the days that followed, that surrender is not a one-off technique but an ongoing posture of humility and dependence upon God.

"Have no malice towards anyone and consider no one your enemy." Neville had already experienced the grace to forgive and to love those who had betrayed him and led to his ignominious transfer to Vavuniya. This current challenge was of a different order—there were people aiming to kill him and the men under his care—but the responses of his heart were still fashioned by love. As Neville leaned into his Savior, supernatural compassion and love flooded in, drowning out the old-Adam clamors for fear-driven retaliation and self-protection.

I learned from Neville that *leaning into Jesus* is the key to living in freedom from the reactive shackles of our old nature. It is a heart attitude of leaning, abiding, and looking unto Him[6] to be our everything, including a supernatural capacity to extend forgiveness and blessing in situations that may be impossible in our own strength.

"Just trust in Me and lean on Me and I shall be unto you all you need for the moment." From early on in his Christian life, Neville discovered the wisdom of trusting God for the need of the moment. What worked yesterday may not be as effective tomorrow. The Israelites were instructed to collect just enough manna for their needs of the day; if they kept it over to the next day, the manna would go rancid and be inedible. This is such a vivid message for us who are now offered access to the heavenly manna—Jesus. We are called to draw all our nourishment from Him daily, to hearken to His words daily, and not to rely on any past "formula," so to speak, however fruitful it might have been at the time. This all points to God's desire for close, ongoing fellowship with us. From that intimacy of relationship, we are in a position to receive whatever we need for any particular moment.

"I shall never leave you, never forsake you. You shall neither stumble, nor lack for courage or wisdom, for I go with you. Fear for nothing." These powerful words of reassurance resonated through Neville, imparting a quality of energy and clarity that lifted him into the Light and dispelled the fear and anxiety that had been hauling him downwards. We all have this invitation from God—to look to the Light that dispels darkness. And this Light is a person: Jesus said, "I am the Light of the world. He who follows Me will not be walking in the dark, but will have the Light which is Life" (John 8:12, AMPC).

I never asked Neville if he had heard an audible voice. I believe it was more likely to have been a very strong impression as he waited in the silence. That is how God continued to speak with Neville throughout the rest of his life—within the deep silence of his heart.

This hearing was not always an "easy" process, though. Neville disciplined himself to be able to hear. Or, to put it another way, to be able to

---

6   "He who abides in Me, and I in him, bears much fruit" (John 15:5); "Let us run
      with endurance the race that is set before us, looking unto Jesus" (Heb. 12:1–2).

receive impressions from God. He would sit quietly in prayer, meditating on Scripture, remaining in communion with Him, worshipping Him. Often, he would walk and pray out loud. One of the most precious things that Neville and I did together was to go out for walks with the specific intention of listening to the Lord. On those occasions, the Holy Spirit would flow through Neville in the form of powerful meditations, prayers, and declarations.

The Fruit of the Spirit

During those early days of relationship with God, Neville experienced His love and peace and gentleness in very practical ways. It was only later, when he had the opportunity to read more of the Bible, that he learned it was actually the fruit of the Spirit that had been flowing through him. He had not even heard about such a thing before!

He wrote in his diary:

> I discovered that there is a spiritual anointing referred to as the descent of the Holy Spirit Who bestows the "fruit of the Spirit" on whoever He wills. The fruit of the Spirit is actually comprised of three clusters of heavenly attributes: "love, joy, peace, longsuffering, kindness, goodness, faithfulness, gentleness, self-control" (Gal. 5:22–23).
>
> What all this meant for me was that before I had read about them in the Bible or in any spiritual literature, I had already been blessed with the fruit of the Spirit, through Grace!

Neville learned, for example, that the extraordinary sense of peace that had enveloped him was clearly identified in Scripture as being a gift from Jesus: "My peace I give to you; not as the world gives do I give to you" (John 14:27).

Later, he went on to experience more and more of the fruit of the Spirit. He was very keen to emphasize, though, that he had done nothing to earn or deserve this anointing from above. He wrote:

At the time, I was not a regular worshipper in any church, nor was I pious or holy or virtuous . . .

I confess that all I had to claim for myself as a qualification for the Kingdom was that my ego had been crushed and reduced to dust . . .

In a most extraordinary way, all ambitions that I had had up to that time for my progress through life simply dropped away. I no longer wanted to "achieve" anything in the world except, through the Holy Spirit, to be transformed into the image and likeness of my Master, Jesus Christ, and to be a demonstration model for Him on earth.

CHAPTER 4

COURAGE, KINDNESS, AND GRACE

BY SEVEN O'CLOCK THE MORNING of 5 April, Neville received news that between one hundred and one hundred fifty rebels were mustering towards the east of the town of Vavuniya and were planning to raid the town itself that night. Although his radioed calls for assistance had apparently reached the Colombo command center, no support was forthcoming. He recalls:

> Hoping for help from the Government seemed pointless. As I listened in on the security radio network it became clear that the Government . . . appeared to be paralysed and—far from coming to our help in Vavuniya—seemed barely able itself to survive.
>
> The stark realisation dawned on me that I was on my own. But was I? . . .
>
> I knew that I could again turn to the same spiritual resource which had seen me through the crisis of the previous night. Which was what I did.
>
> And from that resource cascaded the strength, the imagination and the innovative spirit that proved more than adequate for meeting all the crises that were to come our way over the coming weeks.

A group of twenty weary policemen and some local volunteers were the sum of the resources available to defend the entire town of Vavuniya from imminent attack. In the meantime, the government had declared a state of national emergency. The situation was dire everywhere, and not least in Vavuniya.

Finally, to his relief, on the afternoon of 5 April, the government command center responded to Neville's persistent requests and agreed to send some military support to reinforce Vavuniya. It came in the form of a platoon of regular infantry under the command of a captain who arrived just in time.

But even with the additional troops, the situation was extremely difficult. The captain and his men, and the police, were soon prostrate with exhaustion. Going out on patrols by day, and keeping awake by night, expecting rebel incursions at any moment, these men were perpetually near their breaking point. Yet, together, by grace, they did not break as the terrible conflict stormed on long beyond the few days they'd expected.

The revolt, which had begun on 5 April 1971, would drag on—albeit with less intensity—for several more weeks, although most of the heavy fighting was over by mid-May.

During that time, the Vavuniya air strip was used by military personnel from districts whose air strips had fallen into rebel hands. Some took rest and refreshment in Neville's residency before travelling onwards to their assigned positions.

On one occasion, only a week after the revolt began, a young officer was passing through with his convoy. Neville tried to persuade him to stay in the residency overnight, and not to attempt to leave Vavuniya that night. Rebels were reported to be concentrating in large numbers, and anyone trying to leave the town would likely be ambushed.

Yet the young officer insisted on leaving, and, just two miles down the road, he and his convoy fell prey to a group of over one hundred rebels. The officer and his corporal both died: two unnecessary and appalling deaths among the many that were reported on both sides of the nationwide conflict.

The bodies of the young officer and his corporal were retrieved by an extremely brave sergeant from their convoy. He brought them back to

Neville's residency compound. From there, they were evacuated by helicopter, carried on board slowly, with honor, dignity, and deep emotion, by men from their own platoon.

Neville wrote in his diary:

> As the helicopter lifted off, I reflected on the absurdity of violence and war, and I myself had to fight hard to suppress a choking sob.
>
> I could not help thinking about those other young men also, the so-called "rebels", who were fighting to raise a new society—as they saw it.
>
> For their own dead, no bugles sounded nor volleys in salute. Only the indignity of incineration on discarded tyres. True, they were misguided, but they had caught a vision and had a gleam in their eyes, and they were willing to put their lives on the line for it.
>
> The loss of those lives was no less tragic, their deeds no less heroic, than the sacrifices of these two splendid men.

An Ironic Turnaround

Although the conflict was still rumbling on, it had begun to subside in severity by mid-May. At that point, news of the way in which Neville had defended Vavuniya reached Parliament. From then on, Vavuniya suddenly jumped to the top of the radar, and the government began to pour in additional troops.

Earlier, when the situation was dire, not even one infantry platoon was sent Neville's way. Now, when most of the fighting was over, he was hard put to find accommodation to billet *six* platoons of infantry. In addition to that, he had to scour around for sufficient transport to escort a stream of visiting dignitaries who wanted to visit the scenes of action!

One of the cabinet ministers paid a handsome tribute for "exceptional conduct" in handling the crisis. Neville was quick to stress that it was totally a team effort—a combination of various services and volunteers.

Speaking of the extraordinary effects of the tribute, he commented wryly: "Shortly after the Minister's handsome handout in Parliament, Vavuniya was transformed into a veritable VIP bazaar!"

Three cabinet ministers actually helicoptered in to bring their appreciation, which a group of senior military officials took as their cue to do the same. Neville recalls: "Several high-ranking brass from military headquarters who, while we had been struggling for our very existence throughout April, had hardly acknowledged our existence, followed in the wake of the politicians, rather like a school of dolphins gamboling in the wake of a ship!"

An Angel on a Bicycle

Neville's personal encounters and experiences in Vavuniya were most extraordinary and extremely varied—to say the least. One of the closest to his heart was a courageous visit from a dear friend.

Sister Elizabeth Baker was running a community called Navajeevanam ("New Life") in the jungle some twenty miles north of Vavuniya. She was originally from Yorkshire, UK, and had developed a deep love for the people of Ceylon.

Neville had first met her ten years earlier, when she was the secretary of a branch of the National Association for the Prevention of Tuberculosis and he was the ex-officio chairman. After that, Sister Elizabeth and Trixie became very close friends, and when Mano was born, her commitment to the family became even warmer.

When rumors that he had been wounded reached Sister Elizabeth, she sprang into action and took off through the jungle on her bicycle. Riding alone for twenty miles through the jungle in normal times was, in itself, no mean feat. It was rough terrain, and wild animals roamed freely. Now, she risked arrest for breaking curfew. She also knew the danger of coming up against the militant groups scattered throughout the area or—not least— encountering the rigorous military roadblocks.

It was nothing less than miraculous that Sister Elizabeth managed to complete the journey and negotiate her way through all the roadblocks, using her passport and her attire as a sister, which included the cross of Jesus.

Neville recalls:

> When she appeared in my office I was astounded beyond words!
>
> I asked her how she had made it through the curfew and the roadblocks—and added jocularly that I have a mind to arrest her! She smiled and said, "Don't you know Neville, that all things are possible to them that believe?"
>
> Neville replied: "Amen! Amen!" adding, "You know Sister, the truth of that Scripture has been fully demonstrated to me throughout this crisis."
>
> The look on Sister Elizabeth's face was a joy to behold. Not only was she extremely relieved to see Neville in one piece—and without any wounds—but, most significantly of all, she heard and saw the spiritual transformation for which she had been praying for several years. Later, she disclosed that she had felt all along that someday Neville, a committed Buddhist for the first ten years of their friendship, would be called by God as a witness for Jesus.
>
> The answer to her prayers was shining before her very eyes.

Between the Firing Lines

Despite this somewhat celebratory atmosphere, Neville still had his hands full of challenges.

The rebel threat receded as the weeks passed, but there was still a large number of soldiers present. Their initial, vital mission to provide critical support to the police and people of Vavuniya had been fulfilled, and now they lacked purpose and direction. As a result, morale and discipline declined, and tensions rose—this time between the soldiers and local police.

Infighting escalated and got out of hand, culminating in the soldiers staging an assault on the police station. There, to Neville's horror, he found them actually firing at each other!

Strengthened by the presence of the Holy Spirit, he raised his voice and shouted out a warning to both sides to cease firing, then drove his ordinary car right into the center of the line of fire. The shooting ceased immediately, and that put a firm stop to that very shocking brawl.

Not long after, Neville got the word that two helicopters were hovering competitively over the Vavuniya airstrip: one from Pakistan and one from India. Neither would let the other land first.

Both nations had offered to help the Sri Lankan government with air strikes to "flush out" some remaining hard-core rebels who were still sniping at army patrols and setting buildings and buses on fire well into August. To that end, they each sent a helicopter to the area, with a schedule to land, separately, on the Vavuniya airstrip.

The arrival of these two helicopters produced its own, peculiar tension in Vavuniya. The problem was that Pakistan and India happened to be at war over the breakaway of Bangladesh. But through some "stupid blunder" in Colombo (Neville's words), both helicopters arrived at Vavuniya at the same time, and, hovering over the esplanade, neither pilot would give precedence to the other to land!

"At one time I was fearful that they would try to continue their subcontinental war within Sri Lankan airspace," Neville recalls. "However, after they had finally landed, they attended the day's briefing session in my office, where both parties sat sullenly and listened."

Neville concluded a rather tense day by thanking the Indian and Pakistani officials for their generosity in coming to Sri Lanka's assistance. Mercifully, a situation that could easily have escalated into conflict passed over relatively calmly and without incident.

Each challenge he faced, especially those involving human life and welfare, drew strongly upon Neville's newly found faith and his trust in God, who—he kept discovering—was palpably present and active within him.

New Directions

Neville stayed on in Vavuniya, serving there as government agent for another year. Then, towards the end of 1972, at the age of forty-two, he made plans to take early retirement from the Ceylon Civil Service.

It was an act of faith.

He had no idea what he would do next, but he fully trusted God, not only for his own future but for that of his wife and daughter, too.

Trixie herself had been brought up in a Christian family, so for her, Neville's change of faith was a harmonious transition. They started to go to church together, along with their young daughter, Manohari. It was not as easy a transition for Neville's parents and siblings, and this pained Neville, too, for they loved each other dearly. However, they maintained their relationship and remained devoted to each other. With Neville's ego-driven career days behind him, he was able to focus more on his loved ones. He regretted treating family as adjunct to his career before and determined not to repeat that mistake.

His next move was almost as unexpected as his conversion, and it required travelling a far greater distance than that between Vavuniya and Colombo—but this time with his wife and daughter.

↝

LEARNING TO WALK BY THE SPIRIT

Before he was even aware of the significance of the biblical call to "walk by the Spirit" (Gal. 5:16, NIV), Neville had already started to do so. Events had plunged him into extremely deep waters, but instead of drowning him, the terrible circumstances had actually caused him to push even more intensely into God. He knew he had nothing at all to offer in his own strength.

Some of us, like Neville, experience very difficult situations that cause us to press into God and lean into His Spirit. For others of us, the process of learning to walk by the Spirit may be different. But the core meaning of walking by the Spirit is the same for every Christian.

When we commit our lives to Jesus Christ, the Spirit of God does something new in us. He fulfills the promise that had been spoken through the prophet Ezekiel: "I will give you a new heart and put a new spirit in you; I will remove from you your heart of stone and give you a heart of flesh. And I will put my Spirit in you and move you to follow my decrees" (Ezek. 36:26–27, NIV).

God's Spirit gives us a new heart that will trust Him and live in line with His will. We can never do that in our own strength, but God makes all the provision we need to follow the leading of our new hearts. In order to do that, He lifts us out of one realm (the fallen world) and translates us into a completely new realm (the kingdom of God) which is governed by totally new principles or laws:

"The law of the Spirit of life in Christ Jesus has made me free from the law of sin and death" (Rom. 8:2). Another translation expresses this same verse with some different words, giving us additional insight into what has happened to us: "The spiritual principle of life has set me free, in Christ Jesus, from the principle of sin and death" (Rom. 8:2, KNOX).

While that is indeed the spiritual truth, we still have free will, and our daily choices will dictate whether we experience the realm of the fallen world or the realm of the kingdom. And our choices can fluctuate day by day as we learn to follow and obey God's Word.

For example, when someone says something disrespectful or unkind to us, we can choose to take offense and retaliate. Or we can lean into Jesus, perhaps quietly praying, "Help me, Jesus!" and then move in the opposite spirit, choosing kindness and a gentle response. That is walking by the Spirit.

Another example of the Spirit-walk is choosing purposefully to trust God whenever fear or anxiety try to bate us. We can counteract feelings of fear, for instance, by declaring the opposite truth, perhaps in our own words, such as: "Thank you, Lord, that you have not given me a spirit of fear, but of power and of love and of a sound mind" (based on 2 Timothy 1:7).

Sharing the Walk with a Friend

Neville's close friend Sister Elizabeth Baker had certainly learned to walk by the Spirit during some forty years of living in challenging circumstances with very few resources at her disposal. She had stepped out in faith to help build a simple home in the jungle to care for children who were unwanted, neglected, or living with disabilities. In a later tribute to Sister Elizabeth, Neville wrote that, together with a few others,

[She] ventured out to be with Christ where he is found to suffer most—far away from the perfumery and the tailored comfort of Sunday morning services—among the sores and the stench, the twisted bodies and the hungry stomachs that Christ knew so well.

There are no lights . . . and no fans to mitigate the blistering heat of the dry zone. Yet, the moment you step into Navajeevanam you sense the goodness and mercy that overflows there. The tensions and the pettinesses of the outside world . . . leave you like water from a broken vessel. . . . No one owns anything . . . except what he wears. Yet everyone seems to have all he wants![7]

The Spirit-walk was evident in the life of Sister Elizabeth. The path she chose was harsh, but she trusted in God and leaned into the Holy Spirit instead of fainting in the face of harrowing situations. The fruit of her walk was clearly manifest in the transformed lives of the children and the outpouring of love that characterized her unassuming jungle home.

The timing of her arrival at Neville's office, and the circumstances surrounding it, were remarkable to say the least. And, from Neville's point of view, I think it came at a critical point in his newfound faith. This was his very first opportunity, since his encounter with Jesus, to share spiritually with someone who would understand, and who knew him very well.

I don't know the extent of what they discussed together, but I believe that their meeting was a source of deep encouragement to both of them. Sister Elizabeth inspired him greatly. He later wrote of "the quality and power of the faith that has moved her," and said that Navajeevanam "will endure for a long time as a testimony to what human beings who have committed themselves to God in faith can achieve for their fellow beings."

---

7   From a tribute to Sister Elizabeth Baker published in Sri Lanka's Daily News on 22 February 1972.

She certainly sharpened Neville's faith:

> As iron sharpens iron,
> so one person sharpens another. (Prov. 27:17, NIV)

Sister Elizabeth's encouragement must have been particularly helpful when Neville decided to take a huge step of faith and retire from the Civil Service. He was giving up the regular income that sustained his household and extended family, as well as leaving a job he knew he could accomplish well. Even though everything in the "natural" screamed that it would be foolish to abandon his career at the age of forty-two, he had a strong sense that he should move on, and he trusted God.

A key Scripture on the subject of trust, and one that sustained Neville throughout his entire life, is found in Proverbs:

> Trust in the LORD with all your heart,
> And lean not on your own understanding;
> In all your ways acknowledge Him,
> And He shall direct your paths. (Prov. 3:5–6)

Neville had no idea at all what the moving on would look like. The social and familial pressures he encountered did not make this an easy interlude, but, in the midst of it all, he purposefully chose to walk by the Spirit of God. While he went about his daily life as normal, doing whatever was required of him, in his heart he was leaning hard into Jesus, watching, and waiting for any signs which would point towards the path that he should take.

CHAPTER 5

AN INVITATION FROM OUT OF THE BLUE

JUST FOUR YEARS AFTER NEVILLE experienced his life-transforming spiritual awakening, he received a letter from an organization he had never heard of before, called the World Association for Christian Communication (WACC).

The WACC's main objective was to bring Christian values such as truth, justice, decency, and respect for all cultures to bear on public media. Based in London, UK, they were inviting him to serve as their director of research and planning on an open-ended contract.

In faith, Neville believed it was right to accept that invitation. So, in 1974, at the age of forty-four, he moved with his wife and daughter to start a very different kind of life in the UK.

The contrast between his former way of working and his life at the WACC was huge, to say the least. Whereas over the previous fifteen years, Neville had been the "top man," in charge of workforces comprising several thousand staff, with a fleet of cars and chauffeurs at his disposal, he was now shorn of all worldly power and was reduced to the status of a nobody, at least in the eyes of the world.

He was responsible for just one staff member—albeit an extremely loyal one—together with a ramshackle little car and a room in the WACC's slightly gloomy office block, located alongside a Sainsbury's supermarket. Not the most picturesque spot!

His coworkers at the WACC were a modest and motley crew of pastors and aid workers. A far cry from his previous daily fare of presidents, cabinet ministers, and other political luminaries.

Neville reflected: "The experience of working in the WACC was indeed a lesson in working the Christ way, anonymously and in humility, as opposed to working the worldly way, in the full glare of media publicity and public acclaim."

Dark Night of the Soul

But his "anonymous" behind-the-scenes life turned out to be rather short-lived. He allowed himself to be lured into talking publicly about his experience of Christ, and he was to regret it deeply.

In 1976, BBC Television produced a thirty-minute program on Neville's spiritual experience entitled *An Awesome Encounter*. The BBC repeated the program the following year, and several TV stations in the US also picked up the story.

All this made Neville an instant celebrity. In no time, this publicity projecting Neville as a man of God triggered a flood of letters from members of the public asking him for spiritual help and asking him to pray for them.

On one occasion, a Rolls Royce pulled up alongside him in the street, and a gentleman seated in the rear got out and approached him to ask if he was the man who appeared on a TV program called *An Awesome Encounter* a few days earlier. When Neville said yes, the gentleman pulled out a card from his wallet and asked him for his autograph.

Neville recalled: "I was acutely embarrassed and even ashamed. That, mercifully, was the first and the last time anyone asked me for my autograph!"

He grew distraught over the unsolicited public acclaim: "I had not claimed to be a miracle worker, or a prophet, or even a healer! All I had done was to declare to the world a revelation I had had of the reality and power of the Christ . . . and to urge the world to seek Him out themselves."

The adulation—and the time it required to manage it—was a major distraction which caused him to temporarily lose his focus on Christ alone. He wanted desperately to retreat from all this "ballyhoo"—as he described it—into which he had fallen, but did not know how to.

"I wanted to run away and be totally forgotten of the world," he said.

The effect of this turbulence on Neville's inner life grew beyond his capacity to handle, and he lost the incandescence and power of the Spirit's presence: "It was as if the Holy Spirit had turned His back on me and I went into a deep depression, from which it took almost eighteen months to emerge."

Deep anguish of soul was not new to Neville. He had suffered greatly prior to his vibrant spiritual awakening in Vavuniya. However, this was even more harrowing because now he felt he had lost touch with the One who had become his All in All—Jesus Christ. And the crisis was magnified because, for fear of infecting his family with his inward gloom, he did not disclose to his wife and daughter the depth of his suffering.

Towards the end of 1979, events began to take an unexpected turn.

On hearing of his depression, Sister Elizabeth Baker wrote from her ashram in Sri Lanka with a suggestion. She asked Neville to see a Dr. Christopher Woodard, a physician based in central London who combined his medical practice with prayer and meditation.

Dr. Woodard offered him an appointment on January 7, 1980. It was a bitterly cold evening, and Neville found himself sliding and stumbling through deep snow on the way to Dr. Woodard's chambers. It was one of the severest winters that had descended on London since records were kept, and the bone-piercing cold added to Neville's gloom.

Dr. Woodard's consultation room offered little relief with its lone, ancient paraffin heater. Neville kept his thick overcoat on and still quietly shivered as the doctor led him in meditation and prayer. Then, as he later recalled: "At the close of an hour or so meditating, Dr. Woodard had assured me that I was now healed, that I did not require any medication, and that soon I will be seeing light at the end of the tunnel. Well, I hoped it would be brighter than the light in the good doctor's paraffin heater!"

Dr. Woodard asked Neville, as proof of his faith in God, always to rebuke Satan whenever he appeared in any form which was obviously not a part of God's will, and to continue affirming his faith in God's Word, regardless of what his feelings and physical senses may be telling him.

Not least, Dr. Woodard emphasized the importance of "waiting" and meditating on God in faith.

Shortly afterwards, Neville's local doctor, who had been treating Neville—unsuccessfully—with a whole range of antidepressant pills for almost two years, finally decided to refer him to a psychiatric consultant named Dr. Dale Becket.

Unable to fit Neville into his tight schedule for three whole months, Dr. Becket took the unprecedented step of travelling to see him in his home in south London.

Most extraordinarily, and totally unexpectedly, Neville discovered that—like Dr. Woodard—Dr. Becket also possessed unusual insight into spiritual matters.

After talking with Neville for several hours, Dr. Becket leaned back in his chair and said: "This is not a case for a psychiatrist at all. You do not have a psychiatric disorder, but you are going through what is essentially a spiritual condition which St. John of the Cross describes as the dark night of the soul."

Dr. Becket explained that the "dark night of the soul" is a phase in one's life when the Holy Spirit, having once touched an individual and given them a tremendous sense of uplift, seems to abandon them for a while, so that whatever sense of pride and personal elation they still have may be burnt away.

He told Neville that, quite paradoxically, the spiritual path is fraught with many pitfalls, the most regular being elation and pride, charisma, and the sense of power. To remedy these, the Holy Spirit administers periodic corrections by withdrawing Himself to a degree, and letting the subject fall to his or her knees, again and again, the more effectively to annihilate self and pride.

Given Neville's personal history, Dr. Becket believed that the seemingly dark tunnel of depression was only a profound spiritual condition which was necessary for his spiritual growth, and that he might well be on the threshold of a new burst of spiritual energy. Dr. Becket said he would not treat Neville medically, and asked him to throw away all his antidepressant pills. He assured Neville that, sooner than later, he would come out of his tunnel a much wiser and spiritually more enriched man.

Amazingly, within a few months of Dr. Woodard's prayers and Dr. Becket's diagnosis, life began to bubble up within Neville again, exactly as they had prophesied.

It was as if the sun, after hiding behind banks of dark clouds for months, had suddenly reappeared and was cascading upon him from on high.

Materially and circumstantially, nothing had changed, but inwardly those dark, forbidding clouds had melted away. He felt as if he had suddenly been lifted up on wings of eagles.

Neville wrote in his diary:

> I believe that the reason I had to go through this dark night of the soul, as Dr Becket had described it, was that, in my spiritual immaturity, by flaunting on the public media the experience I had had of Jesus Christ in 1970, and by getting personal profile through it, I had violated its sanctity and sacredness.
>
> Consequently, the Spirit seemed to withdraw for a while so that I may realise that there was no space for Spirit as well as for ego [meaning Neville's old self-life], and that it had to be one or the other.
>
> Such life-transforming experiences are never to be talked about publicly, even as a testimony, because they attract attention to the human being rather than to the Spirit.
>
> The only testimony one can give is in the values by which one orders one's life, so that the world may ponder the secret behind the power manifest through a person—and believe.
>
> The testimony must be in the fruits more than in the talking, the fruits being love, joy and peace, and in the practice of humility, forgiveness, gentleness, kindness, patience, moderation and tolerance.
>
> In the absence of these fruits, my claim to have had a unique experience of the Christ is simply a loud-sounding cymbal.

Therefore, I no longer talk about the details and content of that awesome seminal experience today, but let my life show forth its fruitage.

Elemental Force

Neville was both humbled and overawed at this renewed outpouring of vitality and purpose. He reengaged with his work, his family life, and his spiritual life with fresh vigor and overflowing joy.

His work with the WACC combined concerns that were already close to his heart. One of the concerns was to ensure that public media—radio and television in particular—were used in a constructive way to benefit society. For example, in the Ceylon Broadcasting Corporation, he had launched a series of radio programs to stimulate farmers and citizens to grow more of their own food to avoid food shortages and costly imports. Now, he had the opportunity to influence the quality of BBC output. Because of his international reputation in broadcasting and his Christian faith, the BBC's department of religious programming had invited Neville to be an advisor.

Another concern that he brought to the WACC was to see that all God's children—all ethnic groups and cultures—were treated fairly and with justice. This had come through strongly in Neville's work with the minority Tamil community in Jaffna. In fact, even during his years in London, away from his homeland, he continued to receive calls from the Sri Lankan government for his advice on the ongoing ethnic conflict in the country.

These two sets of issues framed his main assignment at the WACC: He was asked to develop a global program to help world leaders to be more aware of the increasing power of public media. And, in particular, to be prepared for the impacts that messages broadcast through public media could have on their respective cultures.

By the time Neville started working for the WACC, rapidly expanding communications technologies were connecting corners of the world that had never been connected before. Artificial satellites owned by western nations had started to beam their own chosen diet of television programs, films, and advertising into Third World countries (now called "economically developing countries" or "Majority World"), whose cultures and value systems were often totally different.

Neville's concern was to help strengthen and safeguard these distinctive cultures—which included those of his own nation—from negative impacts such as fostering consumerism and commercialization.

Neville often illustrated his concerns by referring to this comment made by Mahatma Gandhi of India in the 1930s. With remarkable foresight, Gandhi had told western leaders: "We want to keep our windows open to the fresh breezes that blow from your part of the world so that they may refresh and enhance our own cultures, but we do not want those breezes to develop into a tornado and blow down our little mud huts."

Neville travelled, lectured, and wrote intensively to help governments prepare for the tornado onslaught. This included delivering talks to UNESCO (the United Nations Educational, Scientific and Cultural Organization) in Paris, and to the International Telecommunications Union in Geneva. His writings on "development communication" (that is, the strategic use of media and education to promote beneficial change in communities and nations) became standard reading for students doing communication studies in the 1980s. Neville's writings on how new communication technologies impacted traditional cultures also became a key part of the university curriculum.

When Neville looked back, some thirty-five years later, he reflected in his diary:

> I admit that, much as I was sincere in what I was trying to do, in attempting to hold back the onward march of technology, I was utterly naïve. I was about as realistic as King Canute of old, who set his throne on the seashore and ordered the sea not to encroach upon him.
>
> Today, technology is no longer being directed by humankind to serve human ends, but it has taken on a mind and a persona of its own. It is an elemental force, self-propelled and a veritable demon, using the human race to serve its voracious appetite for innovation and obsolescence.

Despite this negative assessment, it is important to add that Neville came to appreciate the development and accessibility of more positive aspects of modern communication technologies. He valued especially the mobile telephone, computers, and email.

Neville wrote hundreds of articles on his own computer, and email became enormously important to us in our teacher-pupil relationship, especially from the mid-1990s onwards.

Silent Ministry

Neville visited countless nations as part of his assignment to help them prepare for the changes in global communications in the early 1980s. His access to leading policymakers was exceptional because of the reputation he had gained through his achievements with the Ceylon Broadcasting Corporation.

During long, globe-girdling travels, he used waiting time at airline terminals, the hundreds of hours he spent on board aircraft, and, not least, time within his hotel room for meditating on Bible passages.

Neville was rarely found travelling without the following items in his possession: a Bible, a devotional book (for example, by Andrew Murray) and a pack of colored highlighter pens. He devoured and scoured his books with concentrated layers of rainbow underlining. It was as though he were living and breathing them. And he was. Whenever he passed them on to me, the multicolored momentum of his insights and his faith were infectious and encouraging.

In the earlier, high-flying years of his career, Neville would have relished the opportunity to converse and exchange ideas with the world shapers he was meeting on a regular basis. Now, however, he politely declined invitations and rarely socialized. Instead, he sat in prayer and meditation, hour after hour. In his mind and heart, he was consuming Scriptures and letting them melt into him and transform him.

I don't know if Neville had read the book of Jeremiah at that point in his Christian life, but the following verse seems to describe exactly what was happening to him:

Your words were found, and I ate them,
and your words became to me a joy
and the delight of my heart;
for I am called by your name,
O Lord, God of hosts. (Jer. 15:16, NRSVA)

The joy, peace, and sense of inner power that Neville was experiencing were wonderful, but they were not his main reason for prayer and meditation. His heart's primary focus was to serve as a channel for the Spirit of Christ for the good of humanity and the world at large. Not because he felt he was anything special in himself, but because he had had a dynamic revelation that we are the body of Christ, and that Christ is living and active on earth through us—if we are willing.

Another way of saying it is that we are doorways between heaven and earth, and Neville's heart was to keep the door open as wide as possible for the Holy Spirit to flow through and bring healing and transformation.

For Neville, meditation was the most effective form of evangelism, undertaken silently and anonymously. In that way, he could channel the Spirit into the life of the world without coming into conflict with anyone, and not least, without exposing himself to the risks of rebuilding his old nature—the one that had been crucified with Christ.

He was more aware than ever that his old nature would jump into the driving seat of his life in the blink of an eye, if given the opportunity. The only way to keep it well away from the steering wheel, and firmly sealed under the car's footwell, was to fill his mind and heart with the Truth about his New Nature—the one that was fully enwrapped in Christ.

Neville described the sensation of living continuously in the Spirit as similar to gliding over the globe in a balloon, observing the world's turmoil and tribulation below. While abiding in Christ, and not getting sucked into the turmoil, he would overflow with love and compassion towards all those caught up in it. Then, through meditation and intercessory prayer, he would release the love of Christ—by faith—seeking to open the eyes of people, bring healing to troubled minds, and bring harmony and peace to the nations.

CULTIVATING INTIMACY WITH JESUS

Neville's initial years with the WACC included a long season of anguish and confusion. Gone was the ineffable sense of God's presence and the all-pervading peace that had become the very bedrock of Neville's life. He felt that his spiritual anchors had all been torn adrift, leaving him floundering in deeply disturbing waters.

It was only when he had emerged from this "dark night of the soul" that Neville realized that not only was God's presence still with him but his relationship with God had become more intimate. By faith he knew that Jesus is always intimately present by His Spirit—closer than our very breath. It is simply our individual perception that causes us to use the words "closer" or "far away," and so forth.

From that time onwards, Neville began to experience the presence of Jesus in a more vibrant and intimate way. The months of anguish had served to dissolve some of the remaining layers of Neville's old-Adam life, allowing more of the nature of Christ to shine through. One of Neville's life verses is "I have been crucified with Christ; it is no longer I who live, but Christ lives in me" (Gal. 2:20). His whole heart was to live in that truth—to be conformed, more and more, to the likeness of Jesus. But he also came to realize that the dying to self, and the revealing of Christ in us, often involves painful periods for the old-Adam life, which keeps wanting to assert itself in us. But through it all, God keeps a tender watch over us: "God is faithful, and he will not let you be tested beyond your strength" (1 Cor. 10:13, NRSVA). And when the going gets hard, this is God's wonderful promise:

> Weeping may endure for a night,
>> But joy comes in the morning. (Ps. 30:5)

The experience that Neville went through caused him to long for ever-deeper intimacy with Jesus, and he spent much time contemplating the beauty of Christ's kingdom as revealed in the Bible.[8] Neville's ongoing prayer was for His kingdom to come, and for His will to be done on earth, as it is in heaven.

What Does Intimacy Look Like?

An essential part of intimacy is getting to know God through His Word. A good way to gain insight into God's multifaceted nature is to study the names of God and their meanings. Every truth we discover about God's names and nature is true about Jesus because He is "the radiance of God's glory and the exact representation of his being" (Heb. 1:3, NIV). Then of course we meet the person of Jesus in the Gospels, and, in the subsequent pages of the New Testament, we discover descriptions of the wondrous New Creation life that He has made available to us.

The apostle Paul gives us insight into cultivating intimacy with Christ in his letters. He writes, "Let us keep our eyes fixed on Jesus" (Heb. 12:2, GNT). This brings to mind the supreme desire of King David, some one thousand years earlier, which was to gaze upon the Lord:

> One thing I ask from the LORD,
> this only do I seek:
> that I may dwell in the house of the LORD
> all the days of my life,
> to gaze on the beauty of the LORD. (Ps. 27:4, NIV)

Neither men were meaning a physical gaze, of course. Rather, they were speaking of an attitude of heart. Fixing our eyes on Jesus, or gazing at Him, means to keep Him in our hearts by thinking of Him. It can be reflecting on His beautiful qualities, or on verses of Scripture. It can be communing

---

8   Passages on the beauty of the kingdom include these from Isaiah: 11:6–9; 25:8; 35:5–6; 40:3–5; 40:10–11; 41:18; 42:1–9; 51:1–6; 61:1–3; 61:10–11; 65:17–25; and these from Revelation: 21:1–5; 21:22–27; 22:1–5.

with Him through prayer and words of adoration throughout the day. It can be singing and worshipping in different ways.

Elsewhere in his letters, Paul continues the theme, urging us to "seek those things which are above, where Christ is, sitting at the right hand of God. Set your mind on things above, not on things on the earth" (Col. 3:1–2).

As we grow to know Him, more and more, the beauty of Christ draws our hearts and enables us to exercise our wills. For it is an act of will to gaze upon Him, and to walk by faith and not by sight. Sometimes, the circumstances in our lives are screaming for us to gaze, instead, at "things on the earth," and we do need to glance at those, and attend to them, of course. But the grace to deal with difficult circumstances comes from persuading ourselves to look away from our problems and to lean hard into the One who is wisdom and who is the answer.

It is heart-melting to realize that God Himself desires ongoing and intimate fellowship with each one of us, regardless of our circumstances or what we have done in life. Jesus Himself expressed this desire in the very last prayer he uttered before His arrest. He said, "Father, I want those you have given me to be with me where I am" (John 17:24, NIV).

It is almost incomprehensible that the God of the universe should condescend to desire fellowship with us. Apostle Paul realized this dilemma, and he helps us to see that it is by an act of our will that we enter into this fellowship: "consider yourselves . . . alive to God [living in unbroken fellowship with Him] in Christ Jesus" (Rom. 6:11, AMPC; brackets in original). The original Greek word translated "consider" is actually an accounting term meaning to "reckon" or "calculate." Paul knew that we need to exercise our minds to take in this extraordinary truth by faith.

Then, as we keep reckoning, God will cause this to come alive in our hearts, if we keep them open to Him. Our minds cannot grasp the truth that Jesus died in order to be united with us for ever—but our spirits can. Our spirits are hardwired to grasp it! Furthermore, Paul reassures us that God Himself is the one who will accomplish this in us: "God is faithful, by whom you were called into the fellowship of His Son, Jesus Christ our Lord" (1 Cor. 1:9).

We were created for fellowship, for intimacy and worship. As we gaze at Jesus, in the Scriptures, our minds and hearts will go in the direction of our dominant thoughts and attitudes. In his well-known commentary, Matthew Henry describes our action and attitude of gazing or beholding in this way:

> We must in righteousness . . . by faith behold God's face and set him always before us, must entertain ourselves from day to day with the contemplation of the beauty of the Lord; and, when we awake every morning, we must be satisfied with his likeness set before us in his word, and with his likeness stamped upon us by his renewing grace.[9]

---

9   Commentary on Psalm 17:15 from Matthew Henry's Commentary on the Whole Bible: Complete and Unabridged in One Volume (Peabody: Hendrickson, 1994), 765.

CHAPTER 6

NURTURING AN ALBATROSS

NEVILLE'S FIRST TEN YEARS OF service with the WACC were physically and mentally demanding, because his speaking engagements meant that he was often away from home. During those years, he greatly missed his wife Trixie and daughter Manohari.

His itinerant existence afforded one particular advantage, however: it offered him unusually long and undisturbed periods of time to immerse himself in the Bible and in prayer. As a result, he was overflowing with the things of God and more than ready to share the Living Waters that poured out from within him. When at home, he would share privately with his friends and family. They worshipped with a local Pentecostal community; and also at London's Kensington Temple—a larger, international fellowship. He was often heard singing Pentecostal choruses while waiting for the kettle to boil in the kitchen at the WACC. One of his absolute favorites was: "There is power, power, wonder-working power in the precious blood of the Lamb."[10]

Although he was well equipped to preach and teach the Word of God, and even though his WACC work focused mainly on lecturing and teaching, he never felt called to apply his gift of teaching to the area of spiritual matters—other than when sharing Truth in informal gatherings with family and friends. But that situation was about to change—in a very unexpected way.

Meanwhile, six miles away from Neville's office, in my little apartment in north-west London, I happened to have applied for the job of information

---

10   "There Is Power in the Blood" by Lewis E. Jones, 1899.

coordinator for the WACC and editor of their newsletter. They offered me the position and I accepted, albeit with trepidation because I could see that its scope far exceeded my limited experience as a writer and baby Christian.

I recall riding apprehensively on the top of one of London's tall, red double-decker buses, heading for the association's offices in the west of the city, near the River Thames. As the bus trundled along in the traffic, I can clearly remember praying "Lead me to the rock that is higher than I." I think I learned only later that these wonderful words come from Psalm 61.

I'm sure I had no idea of the significance of that prayer, at the time. Looking back on the occasion, though, I can see how the Lord was leading me and starting to draw me deeper into Himself—into the eternal Rock.

And, unbeknown to me, I was also being led to someone who would prove to be my temporal rock and mentor—Neville Jayaweera.

We worked in different sections of the WACC offices, and Neville was frequently away, so it took some weeks for us to become acquainted. We gradually developed our conversations but at the beginning, I felt I had very little in common with this extremely accomplished man.

I think it is true to say that I lurched into his life rather like an albatross. By that, I *don't* mean that I was someone who was enormously strong and able to remain aloft and steady in stormy weather for hours on end.

No. The fact is, the albatross is also renowned for another, much less poetic, characteristic: this bird finds it *really* difficult to get airborne. It is often seen pounding along the ground in an extremely labored way, pitching from side to side, wings outstretched, straining for lift off—only to enjoy a moment or two in the air before crashing back down to earth in a most ungainly fashion. But it doesn't give up. It shakes off the dust, grits its beak, and tries again . . . and again.

This is a fairly accurate description of the woman who was about to become Neville's permanent pupil. Indeed, in the years that followed, one of Neville's favorite nicknames for me was "Albie the albatross."

When we met, I was thirty, Neville's junior by twenty-two years, and certainly his junior in spiritual terms. The Lord had rescued me from a chaotic, depressive lifestyle just twelve months earlier, and I was still a very long way from lift off!

Even in those few months, though, my vision for life had radically changed. Up until that time, I had been working as a freelance journalist, but it was not fulfilling, and I had soon begun to long for more meaningful and committed employment.

Distinctive from the Start

From early on in our work together at the WACC, I noticed something unusual about Neville. He would bow his head, briefly but distinctly, on entering a room to converse. I learned later that he was committing his thoughts and words to Christ.

Our personalities and life experiences were totally different. At the age of forty-three (and I met him when he was fifty-three), Neville already had a jaw-dropping CV. By the time he joined the WACC, he was in demand internationally as a speaker, and was as much at home in a BBC interview as he was when telephoned by the Sri Lankan president for advice on dealing with the ongoing ethnic conflict. I was the complete opposite to all of the above. I was inexperienced, hesitant, tongue-tied, and confused about so many things.

Neville told me later in our relationship that, despite outer appearances, he had discerned in me a deep spiritual searching. This resonated strongly with his own search for the deeper things of God, and he sensed—very early on—that the Lord Himself had ordained our teacher-pupil relationship.

In the months that followed my appointment to the WACC, that rather unattractive office block in central London gradually became the hallowed scene for countless hours of conversation and teaching. As we grew to know each other, Neville and I began to take every opportunity to meet and to talk about the things of God.

Our individual offices were on different floors, so I would usually trot downstairs to his for coffee breaks. Then at lunch times, Neville would come up to me. My office was lighter, and from the window we could see the tops of trees and a bit of sky.

Wherever we meandered in conversation, the starting and finishing points were always something to do with our relationship with Jesus, the faithfulness of God, and the dependability of His Word. Neville and I were both passionate to grow in our understanding of what Jesus has done for us, and within us, as believers.

Initially, I was very concerned about my lack of maturity in comparison with Neville, but it seemed that my questions acted upon him in a positive way. In one of his many humorous and vivid analogies, he compared me with a suckling calf drawing milk from its mother. As long as the calf keeps on suckling, the flow of milk continues. In the same way, my spiritual questioning continued to draw out from Neville a steady stream of teachings and revelations.

There were quite a few hiccups along the way, though. One particularly embarrassing hiccup happened early in our relationship, when I didn't seem to be able to hold anything together on the spiritual path—or on any path, for that matter. I felt like a tree in a storm, tossed back and forth by gales, broken twigs flying off in all directions.

So, when one too many twigs (unlovely comments) struck Neville broadside, I immediately felt absolutely terrible, and wailed: "Oh! Please forgive me! Just give me six more months . . . and I'll be better then!"

Neville was sympathetic, but his immediate response was to absolutely roar with laughter! Six months to make a saint didn't quite fit with the picture he saw in front of him. I did see Neville's humor, which dissolved the tension of the moment, and we chuckled together over the episode in the years to follow. But it taught me to take my pride to the cross of Jesus, and to keep taking it there, whenever it rose up.

Among the earliest documents that Neville shared with me was a rich compilation of Scriptures describing the benefits of Jesus's death, resurrection, and ascension: Why we have to die, how to die, the benefits of death, and the awesome inheritance of our new life in Christ (see appendix B). These formed part of a treasury of scriptural affirmations and promises that had become firmly engraved in his heart.

He told me that much of the engraving had happened as he sat up, night after night, praying for his beloved parents in Sri Lanka, who were aging, and suffering distressing bouts of illness. International telephone calls were prohibitively expensive, and so conversations had to be heartrendingly brief.

It was a very painful time that Neville would not wish upon anyone. But, spiritually, it was also a precious time of communion with God. During those long nights, Neville would pore over and drink in God's many promises of protection, healing, and provision expressed in both the Old and the New Testaments.

Although he didn't yet realize it, he was strengthening and building up his inner, New Creation being. In the years that followed, he was able to pour out freely to others the rich spiritual manna that had become a part of him during those "night watches."

People, some of whom he did not know, began writing to him for help. For each one, the all-sufficiency of Jesus's death, resurrection, and ascension lay at the heart of all his correspondence, support, and prayers.

Among those reaching out were people of different faiths and New Age practitioners of meditation who were seeking God for breakthrough with difficult problems in their lives. With sensitivity, Neville would explain that it is futile to seek relationship and union with God without first going through the cross. He said that if, as some claim, the illusory self (which Christians call the old nature) can be annihilated through human endeavor *without* the cross, then "Christ died in vain" (Gal. 2:21). If our individual self could deal with itself, and attain perfect union with God through our own good works and meditation, then Jesus would never have needed to come and lay His life down for us at such an unspeakable cost.

The Skies Proclaim the Work of His [God's] Hands (Psalm 19:1)

The spiritual manna that flowed out from Neville included the insights that he was gaining into God's universe. He was passionate about studying anything that would reveal more of the nature of God and His ways. Exploring the wonders of creation led him, increasingly, to marvel at the discoveries—and the profound spiritual implications—of quantum physics, which deals with the invisible forces of energy from which everything in the universe is created.

The physicist Albert Einstein, in the early 1900s, made the groundbreaking discovery that the universe is not made up of separated elements, as previously thought. He proved that matter and energy are in fact one and the same, and his work opened the way for later discoveries that revealed a wonderful unity existing throughout the entire universe.

Scientists showed that the universe is made up of immense fields of vibrating energy which all form part of one vast, universal field of energy. Everything that exists in the universe, including human beings, is made up of this energy.

For believers, the universal field of energy—this cosmic unity or all-embracing oneness—is God Himself.[11] Science is only just catching up, but the Bible has been declaring the truth of oneness for thousands of years. Two verses in Ephesians are among several Scriptures that clearly proclaim it: "There is . . . one God and Father of all, who is above all, and through all, and in you all" (Eph. 4:4–6) and "He who descended is the very one who ascended higher than all the heavens, in order to fill the whole universe" (Eph. 4:10, NIV).

Quantum Physics and Prayer

Christians and quantum physicists alike agree that there is a reality that exists beyond the reach of the five senses; a reality which we cannot see with our physical eyes or hear with our ears, but it is the very real substance—or essence—of everything in the universe.

Einstein's famous equation, $E = mc^2$, expresses that energy (E) and mass (m) are simply different forms of the same essence. It is saying that the material objects of our world are actually bundles of frozen energy, so to speak. Each object comprises atoms, and every one of those atoms contains an unimaginably vast amount of energy, which is released whenever an atom is split.

---

11   "By the word of the LORD the heavens were made,
      And all the host of them by the breath of His mouth" (Ps. 33:6).

Likewise, the Word of God can be seen as frozen spiritual energy[12] which, when tapped into and released, can move mountains, heal the sick, and bring abundance out of scarcity. The activity of meditation and prayer is the spiritual equivalent of splitting the atom. It unbinds the energy hidden in the Word of God.

In praying, it's important to emphasize the need to ensure that what we seek to bring into manifestation on Earth is really of God and of the Holy Spirit, rather than of the human mind. Neville's meditative discipline was always firmly grounded in Scripture, and he took care never to work outside God's grace.

Resting always on biblical Truth, we can pray with confidence. We are called upon to take seriously our status as an adopted son or daughter, and a co-heir, with power to do the same things that Jesus did, including the power to command the elements, to raise the dead, and to heal at a distance.

Every command issued by us, in the name of Godhead, ripples through the entirety of the energy field until it is picked up where it is most needed. As our commands go coursing through the universe, somewhere unbeknown to us, someone, or some situation, is receiving them and benefiting by them. For example, it may be that a rabbit caught in a snare finds release, or a stillborn child springs to life, or a broken relationship is healed, or a surgeon reaches the right diagnosis.

Ambassador and Peacemaker

Neville longed to be able to devote himself more fully to a life of intercession and meditation, and in 1989 he felt it was right to conclude his time with the WACC. However, as it turned out, the prayerful, behind-the-scenes life that he had planned was not to be his portion quite yet! President Ranasinghe Premadasa, who had been keeping in close touch with Neville, saw and grasped the opportunity to invite him to resume his links with the Sri Lankan government.

He first asked Neville to serve as his media consultant, and then, in 1991, sent him as ambassador to the Scandinavian Countries—Sweden,

---

12   Simply as a metaphor.

Norway, Denmark, and Finland—charged specifically to mediate in nego-
tiations regarding Sri Lanka's ethnic conflict.

Well, it was not exactly the path Neville would have chosen, but he
felt it was right to accept the four-year assignment. He had been instru-
mental in peacemaking in the Tamil capital of Jaffna twenty-eight years
earlier, and he had since gained further insight into the complexities of Sri
Lanka's ethnic conflict, with perspective from both sides of the ongoing
civil war.

He deeply disliked the pomp and superficiality that accompanied the
role of an ambassador, but he worked hard to carry out the task that was
asked of him. Whenever possible, he would go for long, prayerful walks
in the forests around Stockholm. In these precious oases of solitude, he
could devote himself fully to communing and listening to His Lord.

Some of his evenings were spent at formal dinners, where he found
polite conversation but very little like-minded companionship. There was
a particularly striking occasion at one dinner party, though. Neville told
me that while he was standing by the entrance to the dining room, a man
whom he did not know kept coming up to him from outside the room, asking for water. Repeatedly. This was not a normal request. Then it dawned
on Neville that the man was not asking for physical water. . . but for Living
Water. And Neville was the fountain he was drawing from.

They had this transcendent encounter in the midst of what had felt to
Neville like a spiritual desert. It is a beautiful illustration of how God meets
the needs of a soul who is genuinely seeking the Truth—even in the most
unlikely circumstances!

Meanwhile, back at the ambassadorial ranch, so to speak, Trixie—as
always—provided the backup and kept their home afloat while Neville was
working all hours and travelling between the four countries and Geneva.
A large burden fell upon her to host formal dinners and cocktail parties at
their residence, and Neville was so very conscious of this, and spoke often
of her loving and unconditional support: "I recall with a profound sense of
gratitude the important role that Trixie has played in my career, uncom-
plainingly, and for much of the time, invisibly."

I think they were both relieved when the ambassadorial assignment was fulfilled and they were able to return home to the UK, where Neville took final retirement from public service in 1995, at the age of sixty-five.

He didn't slow down, though. Instead, this was when Neville's "real life" took off, as on wings of eagles. He wrote in his diary:

> My life is incomparably more fulfilled than it was when I was employed in the world. Now, at last I am able to do the work I have been called by God to do on earth, working silently and anonymously, directed fully by the Holy Spirit.
>
> I believe that, by releasing creative spiritual energy into the world, through meditation and prayer, I am benefiting the world, my community and family far more substantially than I ever did while working overtly among them.

WAYS TO FOCUS ON JESUS AND STAY ROOTED IN HIM

When difficulties and opposition come, as they surely will as we swim against the stream of the prevailing culture, we can safely deal with them if we consciously wrap ourselves in our position in Christ, and abide there. That position has been bought for us on the cross, at an unspeakable price, and Jesus longs for us to step in and remain there with Him.

Satan always seeks to undermine this truth by planting doubt, confusion, and feelings of unworthiness. He traffics in identity theft, because he knows that as soon as we realize who we *really* are now, and the authority we possess in Christ, we become a genuine threat to his kingdom of darkness. His attempts to make us believe that we are powerless in the face of evil bounce off us now, increasingly, as we see the life of Christ within us making a difference in the situations that we face.

The truth is that, in Christ, we are a new species of being: "Therefore, if anyone is in Christ, he is a new creation; old things have passed away; behold, all things have become new" (2 Cor. 5:17). We were brought forth through the cross as "partakers of the divine nature" (2 Pet. 1:4)—with

God's very own DNA now pulsing in every cell of our bodies. We still tend to define ourselves as separated human beings with all our limitations, but that is no longer our true nature.

God sees us through His finished work. He sees us according to who He has made us to be—and not our past, or even our present. A powerful example of this is when Jesus strongly affirms Peter after he had received divine inspiration to declare that Jesus is the Christ. *That* was the quality God saw in Peter—not his repeated failures. None of Peter's lesser actions— however low he sank—could deflect the steady gaze of God's love. That gaze pulled Peter through his most desperate moments and fashioned the future that God had in mind for him all along.

It is the same for us. God saw us through the mists of time and chose us—even before the universe was formed—to reflect Jesus and to be just like Him.[13] That is our astounding calling and our purpose as we walk this earth, and as we travel securely with Jesus, becoming progressively transformed into His likeness.

Only God can perform this work of transformation in us—it is impossible to do it by ourselves, of course. Jesus Himself utters words of reassurance when He says, "The things which are impossible with men are possible with God" (Luke 18:27). To enable us to enter the realm of supernatural ability, God provides spiritual laws or principles for us to follow, in His strength. For example, that of beholding, or focusing our attention, on Jesus.

A Glorious Spiritual Law

As we focus intently on the person of Jesus and His Word—in worship and adoration—we will become more and more like Him. This is a glorious spiritual law, as expressed in this verse:

---

13   "For whom He foreknew, He also predestined to be conformed to the image of His Son, that He might be the firstborn among many brethren" (Rom. 8:29).

And all of us, as with unveiled face, [because we] continued to behold [in the Word of God] as in a mirror the glory of
the Lord, are constantly being transfigured into His very own
image in ever increasing splendor and from one degree of glory
to another. (2 Cor. 3:18, AMPC; brackets in original)

What does "continue to behold" look like in our daily life?

Many of us have busy lives, and our minds are full of activities and
to-do lists. So keeping our thoughts on God seems an almost impossible
task. I think the heart attitude is more important than literally thinking
about God every waking moment. Of course, conscious times of prayerful
communion with God are essential to develop relationship. Jesus Himself
modelled this for us; He withdrew often to pray to His Father, and in
between He maintained an inner communion with God for His moment-
by-moment guidance: "The Son can do nothing by himself; he can do
only what he sees his Father doing" (John 5:19, NIV).

We, too, can seek to keep our connection with God by "leaning in"
with our heart. At the human level, this can be compared to being in the
company of someone we love. We may spend hours in each other's company
and speak very little, yet be very aware of being in the presence of faithful, loving companionship. There is a quality about it that could be called
"attentive rest."

An additional way of maintaining our focus on Jesus is to stop frequently throughout the day to utter expressions of love and praise. For
example, short but heartfelt and frequent declarations are great ways to
keep refocusing our minds and hearts on God. They can strengthen our
faith, too. For example:

"I love you, Jesus!"
    "Thank you, Lord, that you will never leave me nor forsake me."
    "Thank you that you freely give me wisdom."
    "Thank you that your grace is always sufficient for me
in this situation." Singing praise to Him—out loud or in our

hearts—is also a powerful way to maintain relationship with Jesus, and to help us to "continue to behold" Him.

Only the Holy Spirit can enable us to behold Jesus, for the beholding is a supernatural gift. And He longs to impart it to us, infinitely more than we can desire it! So we can rest in that awareness, not striving but seeking, progressively, to maintain a steady gaze with open and tender hearts.

The Power of Our Sanctified Imagination

Because the things of God are so "other" to our human minds, the use of our sanctified imagination is a powerful way to receive revelation on spiritual truth. God gave us the gift of imagination in the first place, and we can make sure it remains sanctified—meaning, set apart for God—by regularly committing it to Him, by knowing that we are covered by the blood of Jesus, and by keeping in line with the Word of God.

Most of Jesus's public teaching required His listeners to use their imaginations. He taught profound spiritual truths by using metaphors and parables based on familiar subjects and life events. One of His key parables is the story of a man who went out to sow his seed (Matt. 13:1–23). Others, among many, include the parable of the prodigal son (Luke 15:11–32), the metaphor of the vine and the branches (John 15:1–8), and the parables of the yeast (Matt. 13:33) and the new wine (Matt. 9:17).

The Holy Spirit continues to speak to us today through the use of our imagination. Neville and I found it helpful to exchange metaphors with each other to assist in prayer and spiritual understanding—especially when we ran out of human words! He wrote this in an email to me in 2001:

> In the presence of the Light, the human mind melts and language dries up. It is then that metaphors are given to us as tools for deeper understanding. Metaphors are chariots of God, sent to ferry us over frontiers that language cannot cross.

Here are just a couple of examples of the metaphors that we shared with each other for private prayer, as well as for intercession for others:

The Magnet and Iron Filings

Neville often encouraged us to base our prayers upon this metaphor, which initially appears simple but is profound in meaning and application. We start by contemplating the supreme majesty and the beauty of Jesus Christ. He is the cosmic Magnet, so to speak. His power and position surpass everyone and everything.[14] With thanksgiving and praise, we magnify all that He is, and all that He has done through His death and resurrection.

Then, as Jesus is lifted up in worship, with our hearts fixed on Him, we can bring to Him those things in the world that are hurting, painful, and broken. People, situations, and areas of the world—whoever and whatever is on our hearts to pray for. As we do that, we see them, and ourselves, as iron filings that have been scattered randomly, out of order. Then, as we keep gazing at Jesus the Magnet, declaring His omnipresence[15] and the truth that He works "all things according to the counsel of His will" (Eph. 1:11), we visualize the scattered and broken hearts and situations beginning to rearrange themselves—just like iron filings—in alignment with the Magnet. Our faith is that these rearrangements will appear to us as transformations, healings, and outpourings of Love.

Cells in Christ's Body

The Holy Spirit will speak individually to each person as we wait on Him, giving us images and metaphors that are meaningful to us personally. One metaphor that came to me some years ago, and that remains an integral part of my prayer life, is that each of us is a cell in the Body of Christ, and He is the head. It helps me to contemplate the truth that whatever is true about Jesus Christ is true about us. That we now have His DNA

---

14 "He who comes from above is above all" (John 3:31).

15 "He who descended is the very one who ascended higher than all the heavens, in order to fill the whole universe" (Eph. 4:10, NIV).

in our bodies, the fruit of His Spirit is within reach in us, and wherever He goes, we go.

Another profound truth revealed through this metaphor is that we, the cells, are all connected in the One Body, so when I/we partake of the Body and the Blood in communion, the life of Christ that we consume flows out—cell by cell—blessing and nourishing those whom are in our prayers, and ultimately the entire Body of Christ.

The more we wait on the Lord, seeking His light and inspiration for our prayer lives, the more He will communicate with us in ways that transcend words. Neville wrote these words of encouragement:

> Never be afraid to open your consciousness to the Holy Spirit as He carries you on the wings of metaphor, on to mountaintop experiences which reveal truths that "eye hath not seen nor ear heard".

CHAPTER 7

STORM STILLING, HEALINGS, AND LIFE IN THE SPIRIT

MANY HEALINGS AND TRANSFORMATIONS, AND the stilling of at least one inconvenient monsoon, came through Neville's quiet way of teaching and meditation in the years following retirement from public service. He himself always kept a low profile, but he did share testimonies discreetly with his family and prayer partners, and he gave me permission to make some of them public for the purpose of teaching and encouragement.

Neville was always more than willing to help anyone who asked him for prayer and encouragement. The people asking him did not know it, but I can testify that it was not at all unusual for him to meditate and to pray throughout the night—or indeed throughout several nights—for the need of an individual, or in response to something that had happened in the world.

He also received requests to lay hands on people for healing, especially on the relatively rare occasions when he was preaching, and of course there is a place for that. But his own specific calling was to teach people to understand and to take hold of the Word of God for themselves.

It brought him great joy to see the truth of the Scriptures coming alive in people and bearing the fruit of the Holy Spirit—more love and patience, more self-giving, more harmony in relationships, better health, and a quality of peace that the world can never give. He looked for the demonstration

of Love, which endures, rather than focusing on any spectacular manifes-
tations which may or may not last.[16]

Neville's heart was full of compassion, and he was very careful with what
he shared with others who came to him for help. It was not always appropriate to describe his own, particular spiritual discipline. He responded wisely,
according to each person, and took care to comfort and encourage; never
to imply that their suffering was not very real and serious, nor to place a
burden of any kind.

He stressed that the Holy Spirit works on an infinity of levels, and no
one should be critical or judgmental of the other. We all live and move
and have our being in the one God.

After he had communicated with those who came to him for help, he
would quietly and prayerfully apply the truths that the Lord had taught him.

So Neville's ministry fell into two broad categories. One was quiet and
often unknown intercession for people and situations. The second was
teaching and encouraging people to absorb, and act on, biblical truth.

It is striking to notice how the Holy Spirit would bring to Neville particular people who were absolutely ready to receive and to nurture the precious seeds of Truth that he shared with them.

One such example is a Sri Lankan woman who encountered Neville
under rather unusual circumstances—to say the least!

The Monsoon and the Lawyer

Neville had been invited to preach at the Foursquare Church in
Nugegoda on the outskirts of Colombo during one of his visits to Sri Lanka.
That April evening in 1999, he was teaching on Scriptures that declare that
in Christ we are new creations (2 Cor. 5:14–21) and that the world has been
crucified to us (Gal. 6:14).

It was an unusually memorable occasion, and he later recorded it in an
email to me. Neville's message was well underway when a tropical storm

---

16 "Though I have all faith, so that I could remove mountains, but have not
    love, I am nothing" (1 Cor. 13:2).

broke out overhead. Suddenly, the entire service was hijacked by the deafening sound of torrential rain as it thundered down, relentlessly, upon the church building. Neville's voice was completely drowned out.

Full of faith, however, and responding to the prompting of the Holy Spirit, Neville was undaunted. Above the din, he shouted loudly into the microphone:

> Now, let us apply this scripture [that is, Galatians 6:14] to this very situation which is challenging us. You see that rain outside. It is assuming a power to disturb us and prevent us from knowing the Truth. So let us apply the Truth right now and defeat this challenge.
>
> . . . [T]he scripture says that this whole world, this whole system of evil, including this downpour, has been crucified unto us. What does it mean, to "crucify unto us"? It means that as far as we are concerned this thing which claims right now to be a power in our lives, able to disturb us and thwart us, has been rendered impotent, made powerless.

Looking out at the rain, and raising his hand as if commanding it, Neville said, "In the name of Jesus, I remind you that you have been crucified unto us and that you have absolutely no power over us."

Wondrously, the rain stopped abruptly, as if it had been switched off with a flick of a remote-control button. But most of the congregation were not aware of the significance of what had happened; for them, the rain had simply stopped, and they could hear Neville speaking once again. Only a very few, who were sitting right under the microphone, had heard him issue the command in the name of Jesus.

At the end of the meeting, a woman stayed behind, waiting to speak with Neville. She was astonished by what she had heard and seen that evening, and asked Neville if he was a prophet.

He chuckled and said, "No, I am just a pensioner!" She had a good sense of humor, too, and they both laughed heartily.

Hiruni[17] went on to ask if Neville could help her with a very difficult situation, and she told him her story. She was a Christian, in her midthirties, married to a Buddhist, and both she and her husband were lawyers. They had been married for seven years, but their marriage was unravelling. Her husband had a successful practice in a town 150 miles away, and expected her to join him there. But for the sake of their children's education, Hiruni wanted to be in Colombo; she didn't consider joining her husband to be an option.

She said that her husband was an alcoholic. To further complicate matters, he was living with his widowed mother, who was encouraging him to sue for divorce on grounds of desertion.

Hiruni expected Neville to pray that her husband would join her and that he would become a Christian. But he didn't. Instead, Neville said he would pray for God's perfect will to be done, which might mean that she should give up her job in Colombo and go to join her husband.

He asked Hiruni to read the Scriptures and in particular try to understand Galatians 6:14 and 2 Corinthians 5:14–21, and meditate on them by day and by night. He explained that because of Jesus's death and resurrection, there was no "husband" as she saw, no "alcoholic," and no "tyrannical mother-in-law." He said that Jesus Christ had already anticipated the whole problem and had crucified it and what she was seeing was only an illusion.

She grasped the truth of both Scriptures even as Neville was talking to her, and said she would follow his instructions to the letter.

After the meeting, while Neville was still in Sri Lanka, Hiruni spoke with him by telephone on several occasions. He was greatly impressed by the speed with which she had assimilated the essence of the message. Shortly afterwards, he returned to London, and they had no contact.

However, about six months later, Hiruni telephoned Neville to explain what had been happening, and to thank him profusely for working a miracle in the life of her family.

---

17   Name changed to protect her privacy.

Her husband had suddenly decided to join her in Colombo. Not only that, but he had given up alcohol altogether, and was now accompanying her to church, which was absolutely unthinkable six months earlier. Furthermore, she was reconciled to her mother-in-law, and Hiruni was overwhelmed with thanks and joy.

Neville rejoiced with her, but he was also keen to emphasize that he himself had not worked the miracle. He wanted Hiruni to know that it had been her own understanding of the Truth that had set her free.

He saw this principle working time after time with people whom he helped—where their own grasp of the Truth caused mountains to be cast into the sea.

Pupil in Training

I was privileged to hear about, and also to witness firsthand, the fruits of Neville's prayer life and teachings. I didn't always find them easy to follow but had seen and experienced more than enough to be compelled to pursue them, while keeping my focus on the Lord and trusting Him to lead us.

Both Neville and I sought always to remain open to the flow of the Holy Spirit, and to develop our own prayer lives accordingly, aware that He leads each person individually. Nevertheless, we did find it helpful to agree upon some kind of structure for study and prayer to follow together. This varied and developed over the years as fresh understanding and revelation dropped into our hearts. But our essential foundation always consisted of the Scriptures that speak of the nature of God and His kingdom, what Jesus has done for us all, and the amazing here-and-now inheritance we receive from God in Christ.

We also studied certain themes, which we compiled in Word documents. The compilation was my "job" throughout the length of our relationship, and I loved it when Neville popped through an email asking me to assemble Scriptures.

For example, on 23 March 2000, he was invited to teach a meditation course in a church in Sri Lanka. I recall it was relatively short notice, and it was uplifting to work together on developing the course and researching the biblical basis for meditation in both the Old and New Testaments. That was something I could do that I knew for certain would be of help to him. That was not always the case in 2000. At that time, I still felt our relationship was one-way, and that I received very much more than I could give.

On 28 March 2000, Neville sent me an email that illustrates multiple aspects of our relationship at the time—excerpted below. He updated me on how the meditation course had gone, but the main purpose was to respond to a lament I had sent to him over falling short in dealing with a complex family problem. I felt that I had failed and been unable to think straight:

> Dear Ann,
>
> I am glad to hear that there has been some improvement. . . . We will just keep on praying.
>
> Please do not let what you call YOUR performance bother you. There never was any such thing. The sooner you realise this the better. Also do not let what you call YOUR ability to think bother you. It was never there to start with!!! So why worry over the loss of a thing which was purely a fantasy?
>
> However do give thanks that the mind of Christ is in you and His energy is right now coursing through you. All these problems coming to you are merely your enemy fighting back. He has identified you as a real threat to him and "all his works" so he is targeting you relentlessly. I warned you that these things will come and that your walking on water will not last longer than Peter's.
>
> These attacks are the surest proof that you are truly in the Lord's commando unit—in the Special Task Force—and the enemy will do all he can to discourage you.
>
> But let us put on the whole armour of God and "stand". Fear not, neither be dismayed, for with them is but the arm of flesh but he that is with you is greater.[18] Your victory has already been won. Rest in it.

18   See 2 Chronicles 32:7–8.

I quote back to you the scripture you gave me from Isaiah 41 and additionally I ask you to read Isaiah 42:5–9.

Also please read and meditate on Psalm 103.[19] You will notice that it addresses "all that is within me"—take the words of the psalm, turn inwards and speak to all that is within you—to every cell, to every brain cell, to every neurone, every synapse and to every neurotransmitter in your brain—yes—command everything that is within you to praise the Lord, for He has forgiven them all their sins and healed all their infirmities—whose infirmities?—the infirmities of all that is within you. Take power and authority in Jesus' name, take the whole armour of God, and command all that is within you in the words of the psalm. Bind the devil and all his works and nail them to the cross.

The claim that you are unable to think logically is a pure fantasy raised by Satan. Your communication to me belies that claim.

The seminar on meditation on the 23rd went off even better than expected and the participants have asked for another which I have agreed to do on the 4th—from 12.30 to 15.30 GMT. They are all fired up with the thought that the Risen Christ is within them and they are wondering why all these years no one told them!! So now they want to know how to access Him through meditation. Thanks a lot for your prayers.

Love to you both,

Neville

I share the email above because it is a good example of how Neville mentored me, and others. He combined firm Bible-based direction with empathy and encouragement. I also share it to encourage any readers who may be feeling as I was! Going back to the albatross analogy of chapter 6: I did enjoy short periods of uplift, but never seemed to be able to remain

---

19 In appendix C, this paragraph is reformatted for use as a stand-alone exhortation for healing. The appendix also includes the words of Psalm 103:1–5.

in the thermals of Spirit for any length of time. Even then, in March 2000. Sixteen whole years after I had first met Neville.

I'm grateful for Neville's wisdom and kindness that overcame any sense of distance and sustained our relationship. But it did feel very one-way, especially in the early years, when I would hear him pray and share insights into the Bible while I just seemed to sit there like a plum pudding—absorbing the cream, but not giving back very much at all.

My growth appeared to be painfully slow. But now, looking back, I can see how God was changing me on the inside. Old attitudes and hang-ups were being reframed in His Light.

Painful Kidneys and Recurring Bronchitis

It was wonderful, too, to see the impact of Neville's teaching and spiritual support on others who asked for his help. One Sri Lankan-based friend, Zerney, had come to know about the powerful healing and transforming effects of Neville's prayer life, and he wanted very much to learn more about it.

Although Zerney and I never met in person, we came to know of each other through Neville, and were happy for Neville to copy some of his personal teaching emails to both of us. Below is one such series of personal messages which benefited both Zerney and myself.

It is important to mention that Neville knew us both very well, and that his exhortations rested upon the teachings that he had already shared with us. He wrote differently to different people—sensitive to the needs and understanding of each person.

For Zerney and myself, among others, Neville took great care to lay a firm foundation of biblical truths before writing any messages such as the one below. That included teaching us that in Christ we are new creations,[20] and that on Calvary Jesus rescued us from the old order of darkness and

---

20   "If anyone is in Christ, he is a new creation; old things have passed away; behold, all things have become new" (2 Cor.5:17).

translated us into His glorious life of grace in the Spirit.[21] Other keys are that the world has been crucified to us[22] and therefore has no claim upon us, that Jesus Himself took every aspect of the curse that stood against us,[23] and He took upon Himself our sicknesses and diseases.[24] Then, by His grace, Jesus gives us His authority for us to exercise over all the power of the enemy.[25]

In mid-February 2003, Zerney asked Neville for help in applying these truths. A scan had revealed that Zerney had an enlarged kidney, and there was concern that he may have an ulcer or kidney stones, or something worse. He was in acute discomfort, and fear was beginning to grip his heart. In the midst of this escalating situation, he reached out to Neville for spiritual support. This was Neville's response:

> Dear Zerney,
>
> I was getting worried about your long silence when your two emails arrived today.
>
> All these claims about your kidneys and your stomach are the enemy saying to you, "Don't you believe this stuff about Jesus Christ crucifying the world and redeeming you and placing Himself within you. You can see that I am still in power and

---

21 "[T]he new spiritual principle of life 'in' Christ lifts me out of the old vicious circle of sin and death" (Rom. 8:2, PHILLIPS); "you are not under law but under grace" (Rom. 6:14); "He has delivered us from the power of darkness and conveyed us into the kingdom of the Son of His love" (Col. 1:13).

22 "God forbid that I should boast except in the cross of our Lord Jesus Christ, by whom the world has been crucified to me, and I to the world" (Gal. 6:14).

23 "Christ has redeemed us from the curse of the law, having become a curse for us" (Gal. 3:13)

24 "He cast out the spirits with a word, and healed all who were sick, that it might be fulfilled which was spoken by Isaiah the prophet, saying: 'He Himself took our infirmities / And bore our sicknesses'" (Matt. 8:16–17).

25 "Behold, I give you the authority to trample on serpents and scorpions, and over all the power of the enemy, and nothing shall by any means hurt you" (Luke 10:19).

I can do with you whatever I wish. So kneel down before me and acknowledge that I am Lord."

In the face of this claim, your response must never be to declare war on the enemy, get astride your stallion and ride into battle. That is what most believers do. That will only give the enemy great satisfaction because thereby you are conceding that he is still a power, as he claims to be. Victors do not go into battle against their defeated enemy!

Then what should be your reaction?

First, just firmly remind the enemy that he has been defeated, that your Lord has drained all your sins and that there are no debts (sins) outstanding and that he is making a bogus claim. Say that you refuse to be duped and will not agree to a double payment, because Jesus has not only paid up all your debts but has in fact paid in advance and over and above the actual amount you owe. So, you simply say, "You are a liar and an impostor, get away! Leave me and my household."

Having done that you turn quietly within, to your indwelling Lord, and tell Him, "Lord every time the enemy makes a claim I shall use it as an opportunity for me to thank You for what You have done.

"Lord! Here and now, I give You thanks that You have taken upon Yourself all my sins, You have crucified the old man in me and You have supplanted him with the New Man, Your own Spirit. Thank You, Lord. This body is now Yours. It is Your Temple.

"This body is now the instrument through which You reveal Yourself. Your Life is perfect. It is not subject to disease, decay or death. I believe, Lord, that as I continue to acknowledge Your indwelling presence, and thank You, Your eternal life will reveal itself in and through my body.

"I believe that Your flesh and Your blood are now a part of my own body and like You said, it is the lump of yeast in the dough; it is the seed of the Kingdom within me, and that what used to be my body is no longer my body, but Yours.

"Lord, all I ask is that You reveal Yourself in, through, and as this body and then all these claims about diseased organs will disappear. In Your presence the earth melts and mountains run like wax.

"Let the earth that is my gastritis and the mountains that are the various afflictions of my body, melt and run like wax in Your presence."

Do this every time you feel inclined to think about your ailments. That was what Jesus meant when He told His disciples, "This man's ailment was not because his parents or his ancestors had sinned but that I may be glorified".

Use every ailment and every problem as a platform from which to thank Jesus for His Death and Resurrection. Thereby the Death and Resurrection will be translated into your own life as your freedom from whatever is oppressing you.

Meanwhile just continue to take your normal treatment. Very soon you will find that the need for treatment has disappeared.

However, you must avoid slipping into the dualistic mode of prayer of the Old Testament for thereby you nullify all that I have told you above. . . .

I continue to uphold you and claim the Death and Resurrection on your behalf, daily, morning and evening, and as many times as possible in between. However, you know the old adage about taking a horse to the water!

Yours affectionately,

Neville

Zerney then went forward for a battery of tests, and found himself being passed on to a specialist in endoscopy, then on to a urologist, among others. Several days passed with heavy discomfort in his stomach, and he found it difficult to sleep. He couldn't think straight, and his mind began to wander when he tried to read the Bible. His wife, Beryl, sat by his bed-side and they prayed together, but it was difficult because they both felt very emotional.

It helped when they played a cassette with worship songs based upon Scripture. One chorus in particular spoke to Zerney: "For He sent Jesus to free us—from sin and diseases. He has redeemed us from death and hell by His mighty blood—so come and Praise Him." After that, he was able to sleep a little before going in for his final test.

The results came through quickly, and the doctor called Zerney with the astonishing news that they could find nothing wrong at all with his intestines, kidneys, or related organs. No hint of an ulcer or of any other disorder, anywhere.

Zerney was overjoyed and promptly emailed Neville with the wonderful news:

> Dear Neville,
>
> I want to thank you for your most encouraging messages which kept us on track . . .
>
> That portion of our body being Christ did not strike me so forcefully. How many times I have read 1 Corinthians 6:19 that tells us that we are not our own, but bought at a price, therefore honour God with your body.
>
> I made the mistake of always reading it in the context of the need to ensure that our body was not lent to any sinful activity, but missed out completely what you hammered in[,] that the body contains the flesh and blood of Christ and there-fore there cannot be any infirmities that can exist in it. That was a great revelation.
>
> Beryl and I will always remember you with love and affec-tion for leading us to the true light of what God has revealed. Coming out of the endoscopy test I was walking ten feet tall. Gone were all the anxieties and the feeling of listlessness and weakness. . . . God be praised for His faithfulness and love. . . .

God bless you, Neville and Trixie. We love you.

Affectionately,

Zerney

It was certainly uplifting and faith-building to hear of the experiences of Zerney, Hiruni, and others whose lives were being transformed by God through coming alive to the truth and power of His Word. Together with them, I also benefited hugely from Neville's prayerful teaching, including healing from severe, recurring bronchitis.

From childhood, I had suffered from chronic lung infections, which had left a scar on my lungs. "They will always be a weak spot," I had been told. Sure enough, heavy bouts of bronchitis, and occasionally pneumonia, would arrive like clockwork every winter, year after year.

Each time, I took antibiotics to cure the infection, but I was still obliged to take time off work, and it always took several weeks before my full strength returned.

With Neville's encouragement, I meditated on the wealth of Scriptures that describe our new identity (see appendix B). I gradually grasped hold of the truth that I am a completely new creation in Christ—whatever it may look or feel like in the natural—and that I have authority, in His name, to banish that lung infection and all its effects.

The bronchitis kept returning every winter. I was dismayed—I'd been receiving Neville's teaching for over thirty years, so surely I should have long overcome this! To make matters worse, in 2017 it struck me down in the height of summer, when my lungs were usually clear and strong. I couldn't understand what was happening. Perhaps I should just try to stand firm and not go for antibiotics this time?

But Neville was adamant: "No! You go to the doctor and get antibiotics—you don't want the enemy taking you out!" I was glad I did because I began to feel very ill indeed.

Then an extraordinary thing happened. The infection cleared up in just a few days, and instead of feeling wiped out and woozy for several weeks afterwards, as I normally did, I recovered very rapidly and soon felt amazingly well. Something was very different!

Since the summer of 2017, I haven't had even one hint of bronchitis—it has vanished completely. I'm healthier and stronger now than I have ever been. As a constant, visual reminder of God's goodness, I keep an empty antibiotics packet dated 21 August 2017 in my drawer. It is the very last of countless such packets that have been prescribed over the course of sixty-plus years and that have kept me alive, also by His grace.

Someone might ask, Why did it take so long, despite having an anointed teacher like Neville? I believe it was because, although I had long been holding and pondering a large collection of Scriptures in my mind, most of them had become stuck there—at the level of my intellect. It was only when the truth of Scriptures started to penetrate *deeply* and come alive within my heart that things started to change.

კ

EMBRACING THE DEEPER CHRISTIAN LIFE

All that we see in Neville's Christian life is open to each one of us. It is true that the way he first encountered Jesus Christ may have been unusual, but his faith walk after that required him to work through the same spiritual, emotional, and physical challenges that are common to many of us. He experienced and witnessed demonstrations of the power of God throughout his life, but he would never claim to be anything special. On the contrary, he often confessed his shortcomings, and he asked for—and deeply appreciated—help and encouragement from others along the way.

Together with his prayer partners and students, Neville sought fervently to honor Jesus's calls to "be witnesses to Me" (Acts 1:9) and to "heal the sick, cleanse the lepers, raise the dead, cast out demons" (Matt. 10:8).

Neville wrote:

> What is important is not just our ability to quote the scriptures
> or have the right theology but our ability to demonstrate them
> in our lives and in the lives of others. . . .

> If the scriptures are not working, it is not because the scriptures are false but simply that we have not grasped the Truth. There is sand in the gear box! There is work to be done, dismantling and reassembling![26]

And I can certainly testify that lights in the Jayaweera household burned late into the nights as Neville sought to deal with the "sand" in his "gear box," as he put it! He devoted himself to mining Scriptures, praying them, and seeking ever-greater light upon their meaning and application.

The key issue for us, as members of the body of Christ, is to become sensitized to the awesome truth that our lives are now hidden with Jesus Christ in God,[27] that His life is now abiding within us,[28] and that we have "immeasurable and unlimited" power available to us through faith.[29] One of the apostle Paul's main prayers for the believers in Ephesus, who were facing extreme difficulty, was for the eyes of their hearts to be enlightened to see and to recognize the spiritual resources available within their very beings.[30]

Just like the believers in Ephesus, we have everything we need—and more—but Scriptures such as these can become so familiar to us that they lose the power of the intention of the Lord's heart. Jesus wants us to be fully immersed in, and aware of, all that He has purchased for us through His

---

26 From an email written to me in February 2003.

27 "For you died, and your life is hidden with Christ in God" (Col. 3:3).

28 "Christ in you, the hope of glory" (Col. 1:27).

29 "And [so that you can know and understand] what is the immeasurable and unlimited and surpassing greatness of His power in and for us who believe" (Eph. 1:19, AMPC; brackets in original).

30 "I . . . do not cease to give thanks for you, making mention of you in my prayers: that the God of our Lord Jesus Christ, the Father of glory, may give to you the spirit of wisdom and revelation in the knowledge of Him, the eyes of your understanding being enlightened; that you may know what is the hope of His calling, what are the riches of the glory of His inheritance in the saints, and what is the exceeding greatness of His power toward us who believe" (Eph. 1:15–19).

resurrection and ascension. This comes by supernatural revelation from the Holy Spirit, who works in our lives to cause us to "know the things that have been freely given to us by God" (1 Cor. 2:12). Our part of the process, agreeing with who God says we are and what He says we have, requires a radical laying down of all previous concepts of ourselves. That is true humility.

Praying from Heavenly Realms

One of the things that God says about us is that we have been seated in Christ Jesus in heavenly realms.[31] What does "heavenly realm" mean? Usually, we think of it as being "up there"—far above planet Earth and the entire cosmos. And that is true, but it's even broader than that. The "heavenly realm" is actually wherever Christ is. It is the realm of the Spirit of Christ, and Christ Himself is omnipresent, as Scripture declares: "He who descended is the very one who ascended higher than all the heavens, in order to fill the whole universe" (Eph. 4:10, NIV).

It helps to know that the gospel writers refer to the heavenly realm as the kingdom of heaven or the kingdom of God. Jesus said that the kingdom of heaven is within us or among us (Luke 17:21). And Paul writes in Colossians 1:13 that God has "conveyed us into the Kingdom of the Son of His love." So we can see that the "heavenly realm" (or realm of the Spirit) is, in fact, everywhere! It is all-pervasive and not bound by the limitations of space-time.

In an email to me on 5 September 2008, Neville wrote of the importance of stepping, by faith, into the realm of the Spirit and interceding from there. He described in practical terms one example of how to pray in that way:

> You sit for some minutes, 5–6 minutes, or as long as it takes, letting your thoughts settle down like a swarm of disturbed bees slowly settling down on their hive. . . .

---

31 "God raised us up with Christ and seated us with him in the heavenly realms in Christ Jesus" (Eph. 2:6, NIV). Other translations say "heavenly places" instead of "heavenly realms." The meaning is the same.

You say, "Thank you Lord, here I am, your adopted son/daughter, whom you chose from before the foundation of the world, to be adopted by you, and now a co-heir with Jesus, through his death and resurrection, seated at his right hand, able to do all the things he did, and reconciled to you, and now One with you. . . . The veil has been rent, and the two have been made One. You are in Christ, and the Christ is in me, and I am in Christ, and the Christ is in you, and we are One."

Therefore you are now Spirit. Although the world still sees you as physical and corporeal, what they do not know is that you are now no longer homo sapiens but homo Resurrectus, or homo Spiritus. You are no longer trapped in physicality or corporeality, but as Spirit, share with the Risen Christ all the spiritual blessings of heavenly places—Infinity, Omnipresence, Omnipotence, Omniscience and Love, and Joy and Peace. . . .

In a twinkling of an eye you can be anywhere your imagination takes you. You can be on the other side of the earth, or on the moon, or on another planet. As Spirit you have absolute dominion, given to you by the Lord, over all things on earth, above the earth and under the earth. . . . However, never will you, or can you, further your personal ambitions, because you have none, but will only make disciples, spread the Good News, and strive always to hasten the Kingdom.

As you float over the physical plane, and hover over any particular person, place or thing, the energy field around that person or place or thing will be electrically charged (spiritually charged) and the molecules, atoms, subatomic particles, Higgs Bosons, etc., will all realign themselves around your intentions and thoughts, just as the molecules of water in a cold bath all start moving around as the power is turned on in the immersion heater.

We have the amazing privilege, as believers, of being doorways between heaven and earth. Between the realm of the Spirit (Christ) and the natural realm. With Jesus as our constant protector, guide, and source of wisdom, we can travel in our imagination to pray blessing and release the healing, transforming power of God over people, circumstances, communities, and nations.

His Love lifts us up and works through us in ways that are incomprehensible to the human mind. But we live by faith, not by sight (2 Cor. 5:7), trusting in the One who will never leave us nor forsake us (Heb. 13:5), and who promises to work absolutely everything together for good for those who love Him.[32]

---

32 "We know that all things work together for good to those who love God, to those who are the called according to His purpose" (Rom. 8:28).

CHAPTER 8

MOUNTAINTOPS, DEEP VALLEYS, AND EAGLES' WINGS

NEVILLE RECEIVED EVER-RICHER REVELATIONS ABOUT the Gospel. He saw that every single declaration and promise in Scripture is our inheritance in Christ,[33] and they are ours to receive. It is a finished work. We don't have to strive to attain them, and there is nothing we can do to earn them. They are freely given to us, by grace. Our part is to surrender internally, accept Jesus's invitation to connect with Him—and to stay connected—and then receive by faith.

One of the fruits of these revelations, and their applications in his life, was the renewal of Neville's physical body. He had somewhat neglected his health during the very intense, early years of his career. At that time, exercise and more balanced living were nowhere near the top of his agenda. Consequently, by the time he was in his forties, signs of wear and tear began to appear in the form of painful arthritis and stiffness.

However, as he went deeper in his relationship with Christ, his entire being began to take on a new vigor. The stiffness and arthritis completely disappeared, and high levels of energy constantly pulsed through his body.

Despite this, Neville was not immune to challenges to his health. On one occasion, I think it was in the 1980s, Neville suddenly fell seriously ill with malaria. He told me later that he was so unwell that all he could do was to lie in his hospital bed and think of Psalm 23. He visualized himself as a

---

33 "For no matter how many promises God has made, they are "Yes" in Christ" (2 Cor. 1:20).

sheep resting in the arms of his Shepherd while the Lord caressed and reassured him back to health. It was a critical time, which could have been life-threatening, but it was not long before he was discharged from the hospital and returned to work as normal, his vitality undiminished.

He was indeed grateful to God for his remarkable health, and the vigor with which he was able to live his life. But, above all, it pointed to a spiritual truth which had become a burning fire within Neville's spirit, which was "if anyone is in Christ, he [or she] is a new creation . . . behold, all things have become new" (2 Cor. 5:17); and "Behold, [God makes] make all things new" (Rev. 21:5).

This was Neville's conviction for others, as he prayed for them, and he was witnessing the truth of these powerful Scriptures in his own life and body, too. He was discovering that the more we abide in Christ and His Word, the more the life of God touches, affects us, and flows through us to touch others.

In 2007, he emailed me a personal message entitled "Life in the Spirit is utterly fulfilling." It was a fairly long message, but I would like to share one particular paragraph: "Going on 77 now, my mind is more alert and active than ever, and my body is in near mint condition. The other day when I went to my GP for a routine check he said he can hardly believe that I am 60, never mind 77, because I seem to be devoid of any of the ailments that characterise men of my age."

This is from a man who would frequently rise around three or four each morning for prayer and meditation, help look after his family, work in the garden, write, and respond to whatever needs were brought to him during the day.

He drew his energy from the One who was his Life Source, seeking as much as possible to keep his mind and heart running on the same tracks as the Word of God. For example, I recall Neville telling me, on more than one occasion, that he had a lot of gardening to do. He stepped outside to do it, leaning hard upon Galatians 2:20 and thanking the Lord that it was indeed Christ who was performing the heavy tasks through him. Neville himself was astonished at how much he achieved without feeling tired.

Such occasions continued to deepen his conviction of God's faithfulness to His Word, and his desire to trust Him, no matter what.

In the meantime, our teacher-pupil relationship continued, and Neville maintained a wise balance between encouragement and correction. Sometimes he was stern, and needed to be. Fluffy comfort was not on offer, but real love was.

At times, real love meant that my teacher would step back and advise me that we will suspend communication for a while. That could be for a day or several days, or, as in one instance, several months. Those periods without contact were hard for both of us. However, looking back, I can see how necessary they were because Neville was so strong in faith and in personality that I tended to lean too heavily upon him. During those times of zero communication, I myself grew stronger and started to stand upon my own spiritual feet, instead of trying too rigidly to copy Neville's every step.

That instance of several months without contact was the most difficult—and ultimately the most fruitful—of all those rather bewildering times.

It occurred some thirty-two years into our teacher-pupil relationship, when both Neville and Trixie became ill. A series of other complications had also arisen, making communication virtually impossible. It was a very strange time, and I still don't fully understand what happened. But I *do* know that the Lord was in it.

At the time, I had no idea if I would ever hear from Neville again. The only report I had was that he was in extreme pain and could hardly move. Emailing and telephoning were out of the question, and my last communication from him had been a barely legible note saying that God would move.

My husband and I live in the countryside, where there is plenty of space for solitary prayer walks, which was just as well. I would sob my way across the fields, pouring my heart out to God while I walked and prayed.

Neville had taught me, and others whom he guided and helped, how to meditate on all that Christ has done for us, and how to take authority in prayer, trusting in the guidance of the Holy Spirit.

There was one particular field which was rich in bird life and had a lovely, tall hedge that shielded me from the public footpath. I felt absolutely free to pray out loud and to move my arms around as I reached out in my imagination to lay hands on Neville and Trixie. I would declare God's promises of abundant life over them, and command the cells in their bodies to come into alignment with their Master, the Lord Jesus Christ.

This continued for weeks on end, and at times this activity seemed pointless and empty. But *Something* kept propelling me on, always drying my tears by the time I reached the sheltered field on each daily walk, and then issuing a powerful barrage of declarations and prayers that really felt as though they did not—indeed *could* not—come from me.

They were painful months with turbulent waters. But at the same time, I could sense a small current of hope and even a measure of joy—deep down, in the stillness of the ocean depths. It was during that time that I began to write a little. I had been assisting Neville for many years but, despite his many entreaties, had not found the confidence to produce my own writings.

Then, one day in mid-December 2016, a most wonderful telephone call came through from Neville. Oh joy! The crisis had finally passed and, marvelously, both Neville and Trixie were recovering well.

He later wrote these words of encouragement—and exhortation—to those around the world who had been praying for them both:

> I want you to know of the amazing power that slumbers in you [meaning, in all believers]—to make things new, to impart life, and resuscitate. Six months ago, I was nearly dead, but you restored life.
>
> That was Ephesians 1:3–23 at work. You can do it again and again. But do not let it wilt through neglect or misuse.

That whole episode marked a major turning point in our relationship. It became much more balanced and mutually supportive because I had matured. And about time, too! I had been loitering in the larva and pupa states of the butterfly for far too long, and Neville was relieved that his pupil was at last starting to emerge and twitch her wings.

At the time, neither of us had any idea how significant this development in our relationship would be. But it soon became clear that Neville needed support as never before. During the same year, 2016, his beloved daughter and only child, Manohari, became ill and was eventually diagnosed with cancer.

This totally unexpected news rocked the family, but Neville was full of hope and strong in faith for her recovery. His physical vigor also remained at a remarkable level—he was eight-six—and during this time, he even managed to write a book about his experience of the Vavuniya uprising, fulfilling a promise he had made to a publisher friend in Sri Lanka.

Trixie and Neville threw themselves into supporting Mano and her family both practically and spiritually, and there were times of rejoicing when Mano experienced periods of breakthrough in her treatment for the cancer.

Neville spent night after night awake in prayer and meditation for his daughter and for other needs that came to him. I used to urge him to take more rest, but he still slept very little. His desire to seek the Lord and plunge into the depths of biblical truth became even more passionate and intense.

Deprived of sleep and proper rest, his health began to suffer and deteriorate rapidly. On two or three occasions around that time, Neville fell seriously ill himself and was immobile, close to death. I do not understand exactly what happened because the circumstances surrounding those times made communication very difficult. But each time, Neville made a most extraordinary and radiant recovery.

Neville told me about one such recovery. He was in pain and unable to move from his bed. As he lay there and communed with the Lord, these words suddenly came to him with razor-sharp clarity: "Get up and walk!"

He knew they were from the Lord, and he obeyed. Miraculously, he got up from his bed all by himself and walked across his room. He was overjoyed and praising God!

There were other times, too, when life surged through him in a most extraordinary way. He would go from barely being able to move to a wonderful state of recovery. And not just recovery, but to a quality of being in which his whole body and mind pulsated, supernaturally, with vitality and creativity. This would be accompanied by an avalanche of emails, vibrant with prayers, insights, and biblical revelations, pouring into my inbox at any time of the day or night!

I could not begin to comprehend, with my mind, what was happening to Neville. But spiritually, there was a sense of supernatural strength, and a quality of coherence which transcended rational thought. The times of physical and emotional pain were interspersed with periods which were truly heavenly, bathed in the inexpressible joy of the Lord.

Another, unshakable sign of the presence of God was that the trials actually served to deepen and enrich Neville's prayer life and faith. He plunged ever more deeply into communion with God, following the ways of prayer and meditation that had been revealed to him thus far.

For Neville, it was as though—through each of these near-death experiences—he was gaining more than a glimpse into the truth that, in Christ, physical death has been defeated. He had seen something that could not be denied, and he was inspired to continue declaring that truth even when everything in the natural was screaming the opposite.

A Seemingly Impenetrable Cloud

The most severe challenge to his faith came on 2 February 2017, when Manohari died. Neville managed to call me, but he could barely speak. He was thinking not only of Mano and of Trixie, of course, but of his grandson and son-in-law, and of his wider family who were spread around the world.

A searing, all-consuming grief took almost physical shape, and settled over the household like a dark, impenetrable cloud which obscured the light behind it and brought harrowing confusion.

In the midst of it all, somewhere, at some level, there was the awareness that the "light still shines in the darkness and the darkness has never put it out" (John 1:5, PHILLIPS)—but in the raw aftermath of grief, that awareness remained very distant indeed.

For Neville, the emotional pain was more than equaled by the spiritual grief that pierced his being. He strained forward, reaching out desperately for the spiritual truths which had been his enduring foundation for decades . . . but now they felt like gossamer. Unable to be grasped.

In email correspondence, Neville was transparent about his struggle. He wrote:

> It is true that Mano's passing away has been the greatest challenge
> to my faith since the 1970s. For weeks I have been struggling, and
> I still continue to struggle like the fly caught in the spider's web.
> I have been on the verge of kicking my faith but I cannot do that
> any more than I can stop breathing.

Even as he wandered confused and lost in his personal desert, Neville was keenly aware of the sacred value of the teachings that had been given to him. He knew it was God's will for others to receive and to be blessed by them in the future. He urged me, passionately, to share his teachings as widely as possible, and to continue putting them into practice.

During those desolate weeks, I longed to be able to comfort and support Neville, but I felt woefully inadequate. We did pray, but our prayers seemed to rise no higher than the heavy cloud that had taken up residence overhead.

Then, gradually, a quality of lightness began to enter into both of us. The impenetrable cloud was starting to break open, as though moved by a kind and gentle breeze. Our teacher-pupil correspondence began to take a different, much more hopeful, turn.

We recalled together that even the mightiest men of faith in the Bible had moments of deep confusion and fragility. The towering prophet Elijah, who was powerfully used by God, became so terribly depressed and confused that he gave up all hope and asked God to kill him.

But God tenderly understood all that Elijah was going through, and He sent an angel with food and drink to strengthen him. The Lord raised him up and blessed him mightily. In the same way, our Father was raising Neville up in His one and only beloved Son who was, and is, his very Life, his Mind, his Love, his Comfort, and his Peace. As Neville wrote during these weeks,

"We are walking through these fiery and incomprehensible times in absolute faith that what Satan has intended for evil, God will turn to good."

I knew he was feeling stronger when he wrote, "I can go on and on, drinking from the Word, knowing that it is the cruse of oil that will never run dry. Sorry for all the mixed metaphors but you've got the idea." I glimpsed a hint of humor in his concern about mixing metaphors!

An especially meaningful breakthrough came one afternoon in June, as Neville was praying and waiting upon the Lord. He sensed the Still, Small Voice speaking to him, and he wrote down what he had received:

> While my faith had taken a terrible shock, the Holy Spirit held me in His grip and explained to me that my faith in the Father, the Son and the Holy Spirit must not be conditional on [Their providing] answers to all my problems as I would have them.
>
> He said that my faith must be unconditional, regardless of circumstances, and that it is such unconditional faith that will turn defeat into victory, and even death into a new creation.
>
> The Holy Spirit even said that if I can maintain that level of faith—but only with His power and by His grace—the impossible can happen, and we can have a Lazarus experience, or the experience in the valley of dead dry bones.

After this experience with the Holy Spirit, Neville's spiritual life began to explode with a fresh vigor and a quality of faith that were stunning to behold. For the next two years, between the ages of eighty-seven and eighty-nine, while helping to care for his family and for others who called upon him, Neville devoted himself wholeheartedly to a renewed life of meditation, prayer, and writing.

This is not to deny that there were tears. Of course there were, because Neville grieved deeply for Mano, and he was also concerned to support and comfort Trixie and all the rest of his family. But he no longer felt overwhelmed.

On the contrary, an overflowing joy and renewed sense of purpose that even surpassed what Neville had experienced in the past began to fill him, and to flow out to others. Each day became radiant with hope: "Let us praise God together for the joys of the day. Unsurpassed and beyond words to describe," he wrote to me in June. "Go now! Drink of the fountain that will never run dry!"

꙳

THE REVELATION OF ABUNDANT LIFE

Although the experience was harrowing in the extreme, Manohari's death did not in any way diminish Neville's conviction that the insights he had received from the Holy Spirit were absolutely true. This included insights the Spirit had given him about the abolition of death. Even if Neville was not seeing them fulfilled in his own life, he had discerned *something* that was undeniable, and he was convinced that future generations of believers would indeed live to see the evidence.

The abolition of death on earth seems utterly outrageous to us because death has been ingrained in the hereditary material (DNA) of human beings ever since it was corrupted at the Fall. However, death was not in God's original DNA for man. On the contrary, He gives *life*, and everything that is necessary to live: "He gives to all life, breath, and all things" (Acts 17:25).

Jesus came to earth to put right everything that had gone so terribly wrong at the Fall. He took upon Himself all our sins and our sinful natures, and gave us His very own nature. He united us with very God of very God!

Another way of saying it is that Jesus erased humanity's corrupted DNA and gave us a completely new DNA. Through this divine exchange, He restored us to our original, God-ordained destiny of an eternal and abundant life.

Neville had received the revelation of eternal life on earth at least fourteen years before Manohari's death. In an article that he emailed to me on 10 January 2003, Neville highlighted God's desire for the life of His kingdom—which is eternal—to be established here on earth:

God appeared in our midst as Jesus, preaching Salvation, Redemption and Life, and not disease, decay and death! He said," I AM *the* LIFE"—"I am come that *you* may have Life"—eternal

Life—abundant Life—resurrected Life—overcoming Life—victo-
rious Life! He preached Life, in all its glory, in all its beauty, in
all its multi-faceted splendour, not merely in heaven, but here
on earth, (as it is in heaven).

The Lord is still waiting for His disciples to demonstrate His
truth to the world, . . . by witnessing to eternal life, through their
own lives. Those who have placed their trust in the Crucified and
Risen Christ have been hardwired by the Spirit for eternal and
abundant life but it is up to them to believe in Him, REALISE the
truth, and show the world! That is what it means to bear witness
to Him!

Neville added that it is important to note that Jesus did not come primarily to fast-track man to heaven, but to establish His Father's kingdom
here on earth as in heaven, which was why He asked us to pray: "Thy kingdom come, Thy will be done on earth as in heaven. He also commanded,
"Seek first the kingdom," whereupon heaven will be unto us an "added
thing." Therefore, an eternal and abundant life, untouched by disease and
decay, here on earth as in heaven, should be the true inheritance of all those
who believe in Jesus Christ. We have yet to grasp, in the depths of our consciousness, the deeper meaning of Jesus Christ's promises, and to learn how
to appropriate them.

Even if we all die a natural death, though, there is never any cause
for fear; we are always enwrapped in the love of God, without any hint of
separation or failure. Look at this most beautiful and deeply reassuring
passage from Romans: "For I am persuaded that neither death nor life, nor
angels nor principalities nor powers, nor things present nor things to come
. . . shall be able to separate us from the love of God which is in Christ Jesus
our Lord" (Rom. 8:38–39).

Still, neither Neville nor I could deny an extremely strong pull to
honor and to contemplate the Scriptures regarding life that had ignited
within us both.

We were particularly struck by the fact that the New Testament is full of Scriptures in the past tense. They describe what Jesus Christ has already done for us and what we, as believers, have already inherited in our New Creation life in Christ.

Inextricably United with Godhead

His conviction that Jesus took every trace of death upon Himself is beautifully integrated with the revelation that we have been inextricably united with Godhead. Being united with Godhead, in Christ, means we are now one with God the Father, God the Son, and God the Holy Spirit.

We have passed from death to life. God lives in us, and we live in God. The "reality" of disease, decay, and death that is so ingrained in our subconscious minds has to be replaced by the Truth that Jesus really did put away our corrupted DNA and that it is His eternal Spirit Who now drives our lives. "It is no longer I who live, but Christ lives in me" (Gal. 2:20).

In an email on 17 February 2010, Neville wrote: "This does not mean that those who believe that Jesus took their death upon Himself will not someday be 'recalled' home, but it will not be a 'dying'. Rather, it will be but a deeper awakening, like the caterpillar sheds its cocoon, sprouts wings, and flies away into the blue yonder as a butterfly, to do the 'greater works' that the Lord spoke of!"

This is an awesome truth that can never be fathomed by the human mind! But it can penetrate the believing heart, and it certainly did with Neville. This heavenly truth saturated his heart with Love, and spilled out through his life and his prayers like bowers of roses opening, blossom by blossom, in the light of the sun.

Neville was convinced that the Life we inherit in Christ has no death within it. As he explained in the 2003 article:

> Jesus did not say, "I am come so that you may have abundant and eternal life, but only after you have first died on earth and gone to heaven".

Not at all! He said, "I have come that they may have life",[34] and He asked us to pray for the Kingdom to come and for His Father's will to be done "here on earth, as in heaven".

Neville pointed to other Scriptures that echo this truth, including these four:

- "The law of the Spirit of life in Christ Jesus has made me free from the law of sin and death" (Rom. 8:2).
- "God . . . made us alive together with Christ" (Eph. 2:4–5).
- "Therefore, if anyone is in Christ, he is a new creation; old things have passed away; behold, all things have become new" (2 Cor. 5:17).
- "Our Savior Christ Jesus, Who annulled death and made it of no effect and brought life and immortality . . . to light through the Gospel" (2 Tim. 1:10, AMPC).

Neville ended his article with an emphasis on how comprehensive Jesus's work was, and an exhortation to meditate on this truth:

After His resurrection, Jesus ascended to the right hand of the Father in order to "fill all things"[35] and so that He may be "All in all".[36]

That means that now, He is in all the 100 trillion cells that comprise our bodies, in all the 646 muscles, in all the 360 joints, in all the 255 bones, in all the 78 organs and in the five litres of blood that circulate through our arteries every minute of the day.

These truths have a profound spiritual meaning.

---

34 "I have come that they may have life, and that they may have it more abundantly" (John 10:10).

35 "He who descended is also the One who ascended far above all the heavens, that He might fill all things" (Eph. 4:10).

36 "There is neither Greek nor Jew, circumcised nor uncircumcised, barbarian, Scythian, slave nor free, but Christ is all and in all" (Col. 3:11).

Let us meditate on those spiritual meanings, and, above everything, believe! "All things are possible to him who believes" (Mark 9:23).

CHAPTER 9

UNQUENCHABLE LOVE

"MANY WATERS CANNOT QUENCH LOVE, nor can the floods drown it."[37] I had often read and heard this verse from the Song of Solomon, and I knew it in theory. But I was now privileged to see it become a tangible reality in Neville's life, and in my own.

Neville and I both experienced spontaneous explosions of joy which were not dependent—in the least—upon outer circumstances. These started to pour in after the Holy Spirit led Neville to his breakthrough in June.

I began to receive exuberant telephone calls from him, overflowing with praise and supernatural strength. Each one was a gift for which I could find no adequate way of thanking God with human words. I recall asking the ministering angels to help me to express the inexpressible!

Such was the overflow of supernatural joy that I remember actually singing *and* dancing at the checkout tills in our local supermarket. A park would have been ideal—much more discrete. But no . . . it happened at a checkout till. I am a (fairly) quiet contemplative and *not* given to extravagant outbursts while grocery shopping—but the joy was absolutely compelling on that occasion. And I do pray that the astonished onlookers received a share in the anointing!

Yes, there was much humor in the joy that overflowed through Neville and myself, but it was also an unspeakably holy time. We both knew that none of this was natural. The sense of the presence of God was palpable and it felt as though our hearts would burst with worship.

---

37 Song of Solomon 8:7.

Fresh inspiration and ideas came pouring in to Neville, and one of them was to tell me—very firmly—to write a book. I must confess that, despite multiple efforts to write, I had been undermining them all by dragging my feet in the ground so hard you could almost cultivate seeds in the furrows. It was Neville himself who hauled my feet out of the furrows and caused my manuscript to catapult into existence. In June 2017, he gave me a stern, non-negotiable ultimatum: "I want to see a completed manuscript on my desk by the end of October. And listen . . . I don't want to hear any more about it until it is delivered."

In just five months' time? No pressure then!

Actually, yes—but it was exactly the pressure I needed. Neville knew me extremely well and he was loving enough to risk issuing such a strong ultimatum. He was obeying the nudging of the Holy Spirit. As a result, my book, *God's Gift of Tremendous Power*, based upon Ephesians 1:19, was published by Deep River Books less than two years later, in March 2019.

Golden Bowls Full of Incense

I knew for sure that Neville was more than restored when a new set of spiritual guidelines came thundering across the country into my inbox on 19 October 2017. No time to waste! By spiritual guidelines, I mean a lively collection of scriptural themes and writings that we could both follow for daily worship, meditation, and intercession.

Looking back over my incoming emails from that time, I'm amazed to see their vigor and spiritual depth. Many of them were Scripture-rich affirmations and prayers. I believe—as did Neville—that his writings were not only emails sent to me but also intercessions imparted into the world. I would compare them to the "golden bowls full of incense, which are the prayers of the saints" mentioned in Revelation 5:8.

I was privileged to pray together with Neville in a two-way flow of email correspondence which was rich and invigorating. And I believe it blessed and encouraged us both.

He would make his way to his computer at the prompting of the Holy Spirit to share what had inspired him, as well as to hear from me. Here is an example from an email he wrote to me on 13 July 2019, exhorting me regarding the Lord's Prayer:

> When the disciples asked the Master what they should pray for He said, "Pray like this" and He gave us the Lord's Prayer.
>
> The essence of the Lord's prayer is "Thy Kingdom come, Thy Will be done". Nothing outside it can improve it! However good or beautiful the earthly version is, it is a fake.
>
> The truth is the Kingdom and His Will! Sadly, over the past 2000-something years the Lord's Prayer has been treated as a mantra with no substance to it!
>
> Let us even now turn things around and treat the Lord seriously and pray as He taught us.

This is one of many times a familiar passage of the Bible would blaze with new light, propelling us both to pray with increased conviction. Neville and I knew without any doubt that we had tasted the glory of God's Kingdom, even though the taste was a modest one. It was as though our spiritual eyes were being opened wider and wider to the truth that the kingdom of God is not far away, to be attained sometime in the future. Rather, it is a vibrant, radiant, present Reality—readily available for believers to experience personally, here and now, for, as Jesus Himself said, "the kingdom of God is within you" (Luke 17:21).[38]

Reflecting back over our years of seeking God together, I can see that the Lord was leading us, teaching us to lean into Him, to keep His Word alive in our hearts, and to not be dismayed by challenges. Each time a challenge or difficulty rose, threatening to snuff out the fire of our faith, it seemed that the Lord would release more and more oxygen onto the dwindling flames, and they would grow back higher and stronger. Back in

---

38 The Amplified version expresses it this way: "The kingdom of God is within you [in your hearts] and among you [surrounding you]" (Luke 17:21, AMPC; brackets in the original).

2003, Neville wrote this exhortation, and its message is equally valuable
for today:

> There are mountains, vast ranges, to climb, but conquer them all
> we must. We have been given the map and shown the paths. It is
> for us to climb.
>
> This means in essence, practice, practice, practice, practice,
> morning, noon and night, awake or asleep, regardless that results
> may not be commensurate with what we deem to be our deserts.
> That is FAITH, to press on, because we KNOW, even if for the
> moment we do not see.

By "practice," Neville meant applying the principles (all based on
Scriptures) he shared liberally in his teachings. They are rich in variety,
but in essence they are simple: love God, love people, love God's Word (the
Bible), and seek to believe it and put it into practice.

I would like to share with you this powerful phrase which I keep tucked
within my Bible and ponder frequently. I don't know who wrote it, but it is
profound and true. The "Word" means, of course, both the Living Word,
Jesus, and His written Word, Scripture:

> "The more weight you put on the Word, the more the Word will
> support you."

A Radiant Encounter

A most extraordinary day came in March 2018. For the first time in
nineteen years, I was going to see Neville. Yes, it had been that long! It just
turned out that way through circumstances and through living at a distance from each other.

After we had left our workplace in the WACC, even though we rarely
met physically, our relationship continued to blossom over email and by
telephone, sustained and directed in a remarkable way by the Holy Spirit.
We did miss seeing each other in person, though.

The opportunity to meet again arose when I happened to be in London and learned that Neville had been taken to a hospital nearby for a short stay. I could scarcely believe that I would be seeing my beloved teacher again. How would our meeting be—for both of us?

I climbed the stairs to his hospital ward with a fluttering heart. I so longed to see my teacher again, and yet I had no idea what I might see. I knew that Neville had sufficient breath to speak, for he had called me on his mobile phone from the hospital. But that was all I knew at the time.

The nurse on reception gestured towards Neville's cubicle—the curtains half drawn. I ventured tentatively around the curtain . . . and saw a most glorious sight.

Neville was sitting calmly on a chair by his bed, and I can only describe him as radiating the Light, the Love, and the Peace of God. We shared a truly heavenly encounter that I cannot even begin to fully convey in words. It was as though time stood still—as though we were meeting on holy ground indeed.

We conversed tenderly together, and words flowed between us, but words were not the most important part of our meeting. There was a much higher order of communication happening, which caused our material surroundings to feel extremely light and full of peace. The desire to ask questions seemed to melt away. In any case, the answers would never ultimately satisfy—only God's Presence satisfies. At that moment, and at any moment, I can declare that *in His Presence* . . . all is well.

The Holy Spirit was uplifting us and, I believe, affecting the atmosphere in the ward. There seemed to be a sense of awe, and I recall one of the beautiful nurses gazing towards us with her face bathed in peace and tenderness. The experience of that day is forever engraved upon the deepest recesses of my heart.

I floated home on the train, in another world, immensely uplifted and in awe of God's ways. Later that afternoon, Neville called me with renewed strength—also overawed and overjoyed by the experience we had shared. It was an inexpressibly holy encounter for both of us. He returned to his home shortly afterwards, and we resumed our emails and telephone calls, buoyed up in ways that are also beyond human comprehension.

The Upward Call of God

Content to be unknown and invisible, Neville's burning desire was always to glorify the Lord, to strive to manifest the life of Jesus, and prove His Word true—at whatever cost. He sought only to declare the truth that he found in the Bible, illuminated by the Holy Spirit, the fruits of which he saw in abundance.

Neville entrusted his teaching, and his everything, entirely to the Lord, resting in the knowledge that "unless the LORD builds the house, they labor in vain who build it" (Ps. 127:1).

His absolute focus—after his devotion to the Lord—was in taking care of those around him, and those afar, who were in touch by telephone. He gave of himself without hesitation. Neville would not have compared himself with the apostle Paul, but I believe Paul's words apply very well to Neville's life: "if I am being poured out as a drink offering on the sacrifice and service of your faith, I am glad and rejoice with you all" (Phil. 2:17).

His immediate concern at home was for his beloved wife, Trixie. In early 2020, she became very weak, and remained in bed. She was eighty-nine. The Covid-19 pandemic complicated their situation, with the UK government imposing a lockdown in mid-March 2020, ordering people to stay at home except for those providing essential services.

Their family and friends could not visit, but Neville and Trixie had constant support from carers who were staying with them in their home throughout the lockdown period. Neville was particularly touched when the vicar of their local church came round to the side of the house, and prayed with him and Trixie through an open window.

Trixie was being cared for in a room close to Neville's study, and he would spend hours sitting by her bed, holding her hand and praying while she slept calmly in his presence.

Also aged eighty-nine, Neville was still sending me almost daily emails of praise and thanksgiving—and exhortation. He was ever the teacher! But starting on 23 March 2020, he needed to rest in bed. The emails stopped—but communication continued by telephone.

Neville kept his telephone by his bed, and used speakerphone when he was resting back on his pillow. There followed an entire month of praying, reading, and singing together over the phone, often several times a day. I'm no nightingale, and my husband was amused to hear me trying to coax my vocal cords into shape between sessions—because Neville favored the higher registers!

As the days went by, Neville's physical strength started to drain away, and he grew quieter. Deeply attentive to Trixie, he asked his carer to help him to reach her bedside as long as that was possible. And he still wanted me to pray and to worship in song as he lay back on his pillow next to the speakerphone.

Trixie died peacefully just five days before Neville, which was most remarkable timing. He would never have wanted to leave her bereft of his care and his presence.

We continued in gentle communion over the telephone. Our calls were precious and sacred times of prayer, sharing, and worship.

Neville himself went to heaven at 11:45 p.m. on 10 May 2020, and I received the news from his family shortly afterwards, at 1 a.m.

Paeans of Praise

Something very wonderful happened before he departed this earth.

For the previous several days, when his carer kindly positioned the telephone close to his pillow each time I rang, I could hear Neville's irregular breathing. We remained together, tenderly, and I would gently speak words of reassurance and love. Occasionally, he would murmur a muffled "please pray"—but that was all. His physical strength and capacity had drained away. He was barely conscious.

So it was utterly miraculous, just hours before he died, to hear Neville literally burst out with loud paeans of praise! Beautiful words cascaded from his lips with crystal clarity—the endless springs of Living Water.

Love that can never be quenched, ever.

The first verse of Psalm 103 filled the atmosphere as he repeated it, over and over again:

Bless the LORD, O my soul: and all that is within me, bless his holy name.

Bless the LORD, O my soul: and all that is within me, bless his holy name.

Surely there is no more appropriate, overflowing, eternal song of praise.

CONCLUSION

SWEET FRAGRANCE

I PRAY THAT THIS BOOK has given you the opportunity to encounter the heart of God—and God's desire for each one of us—through some fairly brief, but very personal, glimpses into the life and teachings of Neville Jayaweera.

As his pupil, what I valued most was that he showed how an intimate, moment-by-moment relationship with God is available to absolutely everyone who chooses to pursue it. Everyone is invited to step into the radiant new life that has already been provided for us in Christ.

Neville had a vision of this New Creation life to be lived out here on earth, and not just when we leave this earth and go to heaven. He poured out his own life to explain, and to start to demonstrate, what it means to be crucified with Christ, to be made new in Him, and to live out the Life that God Himself designed for us to live.

Jesus has died our death on our behalf, but it is up to us to identify closely with Him. As we do, we can work together with God to transform our own lives, make a difference in the world, and be part of ushering in God's will and His kingdom upon the earth.

We are the ambassadors of heaven to bring the kingdom here. We find everything we need as we surrender to Him and abide in Him. In that place, we are filled with His wisdom, His love, His courage, and the power of His Spirit[39] to transform our lives and the lives of others.

This is the Lord's planet—

---

39 "'Not by might nor by power, but by my Spirit,' says the LORD Almighty" (Zech. 4:6, NIV).

"The earth is the Lord's, and everything in it,
the world, and all who live in it." (Ps. 24:1)

—and He has entrusted it to us. This does not just apply to the millennium reign when Jesus returns; it applies to us now. Right now, we have the astonishing privilege of hosting the Life of Jesus Christ on earth and of carrying out His mandate to make a difference.[40]

Neville taught powerfully on the vital importance of dying to our old nature in order for the Spirit of Christ to flow through without hindrance. The image that comes to mind is the crushing of a spice for the sweet fragrance to be released. And in Neville, the fragrance was sweet indeed. I saw it—over and over again.

For Neville, the turning point came during his first year at Vavuniya. The crushing and struggling he had experienced up until then gave way to joy and peace as he encountered waves of God's love. That was the start of his transformation. From then on, while reckoning that his old nature had been dealt with at the cross, he kept his heart focused on Jesus and began to spread the fragrance of the knowledge of God wherever he went.[41] Paul reveals in his letter to the Corinthian church that we can all share in this outpouring of grace: "Because of Christ, we give off a sweet scent rising to God" (2 Cor. 2:15, MSG).

Neville would absolutely *not* want to be portrayed as perfect, and of course he was not. He lamented his failures and knew his utter need for Jesus. But I can say unreservedly that I believe I have never met anyone more loving, forgiving, self-giving, patient, and wise.

He had at least as many opportunities to practice this love and forgiveness in the UK as he had during his political persecution in Sri Lanka. I saw the way in which Neville responded to all kinds of insults and attacks that

---

40 "As you go, preach, saying, 'The kingdom of heaven is at hand.' Heal the sick, cleanse the lepers, raise the dead, cast out demons. Freely you have received, freely give" (Matt. 10:7–8).

41 2 Corinthians 2:14

were launched against him in different settings. Some sprang from envy, some from blatant racism, and some from disdain for born-again believers in general. Really shocking things happened, but the more Neville was squeezed in this way, the more love and compassion flowed out from him in a supernatural way. No matter the severity of what came against him, while it pained him, he bore no hint of offense or desire for retaliation.

He lived constantly in the realization that he had been bought at a price and that he was not his own anymore. He belonged to Christ (1 Cor. 6:19–20). And so, whenever he encountered evil, or a difficulty of any kind, he would recall that Jesus had taken this, too, upon the cross. That the world (and all its evil) had been crucified with Christ. Neville's heart was to see everyone and everything as *God* saw them—through the work of His Son, through the truth of Resurrection and New Life—and not as things look in the natural, however compelling they may seem. In line with this, he would seek to follow the instruction of Jesus: "You must not judge by the appearance of things but by the reality!" (John 7:24, PHILLIPS). During his life, Neville witnessed much healing and transformation as the result of believing and praying in this way.

I recall this email he sent to me on 2 September 2016, when he was faced with a particularly difficult situation: "Whatever the senses testify to, I know that the truth is the opposite. It is just not blind faith but I KNOW, and knowing enables me to smile when mountains bar my progress."

I miss Neville profoundly. But, at the same time, my heart overflows with wonder, and worship, and thanksgiving. Life is full of vibrant hope in Christ, with anticipation of ever-deeper revelations in the spiritual realm, manifesting through believers.

We are the living body of Christ—the expression of Jesus upon the earth. Jesus Christ is walking and breathing on earth, once again, inside His people. We are the temple of the Holy Spirit, individually, and together— living doorways between heaven and earth!

Even in his final year, when he was eighty-nine and had encountered many challenges, Neville exploded with humanly impossible periods of vigor and joy. These were characterized by childlike faith and by prophetic vision that pointed the way to new realities as yet unseen. But we both shared the conviction that they *will* be seen on earth in the future. Even if his own experience did not always match what he believed to be true, he did not stop believing it or declaring it.

He trusted in his Lord, and the Word of God, above and beyond anything that he had seen or experienced in the natural, because he had seen and tasted the goodness of the Lord.[42]

He encouraged me strongly to continue pressing onwards, in faith, and to pursue intimacy with Jesus with all fervency, always honoring His Word and resting upon it. And he would urge every believer to do the same.

I know that Neville would bless you and cheer you on unreservedly as you seek to know Jesus Christ, to shine with His beautiful light, and to manifest His will on earth in ever-deeper measure.

---

42 "Taste and see that the LORD is good;
    blessed is the one who takes refuge in him" (Ps. 34:8).

SCRIPTURES ON PRAYING WITHOUT CEASING

Neville wrote this meditation, together with a short introduction, on 17 July 2006. He edited it slightly on 12 September 2015 and replaced the personal pronoun "i" with "we" to reflect his heart for intercessory prayer. It is still, however, a powerful prayer if used in the first person, and it is an effective way of renewing the mind in line with biblical truth.

This is just one suggested way in which we can follow Paul's instruction to "pray without ceasing" (1 Thess. 5:17); the underlying emphasis being that we seek to maintain unbroken communion with God through keeping His Word in our minds and hearts.

The relevant Scripture references are woven into the meditation.

❦

I thought I'd put down in writing the spiritual narrative I run through in my mind whenever I am not otherwise overtly engaged—that is what it means to pray without ceasing.

Most days I fall asleep repeating this prayer in my mind so that even in deep sleep it continues to do its work within my consciousness, which is when it is most effective, because nothing is there to distract it as it continues to impart truth to the entire body, including those I am holding in intercessory prayer.

In the edited version I have kept out the word "i" and replaced it with "we" because that is what true intercessory prayer should be.

Pray without Ceasing

We were chosen in Christ before the creation of the world (Eph. 1:4). It is of God that we are in Christ Jesus (1 Cor. 1:30; Col. 1:16,17). Therefore, when He died, we died with Him (Gal. 2:20). Indeed, all died with Him . . . [here we mention a string of names we are interceding for] . . . (2 Cor. 5:14). Therefore we shall no longer judge anyone as he/she appears to our senses in the flesh (2 Cor. 5:16; John 7:24).

Because we all died with him (Rom. 6:5), and because we were also buried with Him and also raised with him (Rom. 6:4), we are born again (1 Pet. 1:23), born not of flesh and blood, not of human will (John 1:13) but from above.

Because we put our faith in Jesus as the Christ, we are born of God (1 John 5:1) [and] born of Spirit (John 3:8), and the life of Christ is now manifesting in our mortal bodies (2 Cor. 4:11). Our bodies were only earthen vessels (2 Cor. 4:7), but He has restored life to us (Eph. 2:5) and we are therefore new creations (2 Cor. 5:17), partakers of the divine nature (2 Pet. 1:4) and adopted siblings of the Risen Lord (Eph. 1:5), co-heirs with Him (Rom. 8:17), raised with Him (Eph. 2:6) and blessed with all spiritual blessings in heavenly places (Eph. 1:3).

The life that is now in us is the Risen Christ (Col. 3:4) appearing as [each of us], and He is not subject to the law of sin and death (Rom. 8:2; Col. 2:13.14). His life, now manifesting in our mortal flesh (2 Cor. 4:11), is the eternal life (John 10:28), the abundant life (John 10:10), the exchanged life (Gal. 3:13), the transformed life (2 Cor. 3:18), the life that has overcome the world (John 16:33). Therefore mortality has put on immortality, the perishable has put on the imperishable (1 Cor. 15:53) and we have passed from darkness to light (Col. 1:12–13), from death to life (John 5:24; Rom. 6:4; Rom. 6:13). We are therefore now vessels consecrated and fit for the Father's use (Eph. 2:10).

The Lord has assured us that now we can do all the things that He did, and even greater things (John 14:12). Even though right now, our senses do not always testify to this belief, we have faith that the Lord was not lying (Titus 1:2), and that therefore, as we continue to believe, the testimony of our senses will line up with our beliefs (Rom. 4:20–21).

Right now, our task to is to glorify the Lord on earth (Rom. 15:6), by serving as instruments in the hands of the Holy Spirit (Rom. 7:6), for filling all things with Christ (Love) so that Christ is in all, through all and is All in all (Eph. 4:4).

Because we have given over our bodies as living sacrifices to the Lord (Rom. 12:1), our bodies are now temples of the Holy Spirit (1 Cor. 6:19) and temples of God (1 Cor. 3:16), dematerialised and transfigured with the Lord (2 Cor. 4:11) and therefore pure Spirit (1 Cor. 6:17), sharing in all the properties of Spirit (1 Cor. 12:13). Our bodies are therefore no longer subject to the law of sin and death or entropy (Rom. 8:2). In fact, Jesus Christ, who has replaced the fallen Adam (1 Cor. 15:45), is now governing and completing our bodies (Col. 2:9–10). He is reconfiguring them (Rom. 8:29) and bringing them into line with God's will and purpose (Rom. 12:2; Eph. 1:11), the pattern shown on the mount (Heb. 8:5).

All this, not for our glory but for glorifying the Lord (1 Cor. 10:31) and hastening His Kingdom come on earth (Matt. 6:10). However, sowing to the flesh (or the carnal mind) will undermine and pollute all the above (Gal. 6:8).

The Truths set out above are latently or juridically true of every human being (1 Tim. 2:4), living, dead, and yet unborn, but it is up to us under the guidance of Spirit, to claim them on their behalf (Matt. 9:37), and using the powers vested in us (Luke 9:1; Luke 10:19), to help raise the Kingdom peopled by the children of God (Luke 13:29).

Amen! Praise God!!

THE BIBLICAL PROGRESSION FROM OUR OLD SELF-LIFE TO OUR NEW CREATION LIFE

THIS LIST INCLUDES NEVILLE'S EARLY collections of Scriptures addressing the benefits of Jesus's death, resurrection, and ascension, together with some additional verses that also became invaluable to our prayer lives. The list is by no means exhaustive, of course; it simply offers some suggestions for studying and meditating on the themes below.

Neville stressed the value of choosing to focus upon just one Scripture at a time, then pondering deeply for as long as it takes to saturate and renew our minds and hearts.

The Biblical Progression from Our Old Self-Life to Our New Creation Life in Christ Jesus

We have a glorious inheritance—right here on Earth!

Why We Have to Die to Our Old Self
- "The natural man does not receive the things of the Spirit of God, for they are foolishness to him; nor can he know them, because they are spiritually discerned" (1 Cor. 2:14).
- "Unless a grain of wheat falls into the ground and dies, it remains alone; but if it dies, it produces much fruit" (John 12:24).

- "Whoever desires to save his life will lose it, but whoever loses his life for My sake will find it" (Matt. 16:25).
- "Clearly no one who relies on the law is justified before God, because 'the righteous will live by faith'" (Gal. 3:11, NIV).

How We Die to Our Old Self

We identify with Jesus's death on our behalf, and renew our minds according to Scriptures:

- "Reckon yourselves to be dead indeed to sin, but alive to God in Christ Jesus our Lord" (Rom. 6:11).
- "Our old man was crucified with Him, that the body of sin might be done away with, that we should no longer be slaves of sin" (Rom. 6:6).
- "You were taught, with regard to your former way of life, to put off your old self, which is being corrupted by its deceitful desires; to be made new in the attitude of your minds; and to put on the new self, created to be like God in true righteousness and holiness" (Eph. 4:22–24, NIV).
- "I die daily" (1 Cor. 15:31).
- "If anyone desires to come after Me, let him deny himself, and take up his cross daily, and follow Me" (Luke 9:23).
- "Do not be conformed to this world, but be transformed by the renewing of your mind" (Rom. 12:2).

The Benefits of Dying to the Old, and Rising to New Creation Life in Christ

That is, rising into our new identity in Christ.

- "God made you alive with Christ. He forgave us all our sins, having canceled the charge of our legal indebtedness, which stood against us" (Col. 2:13–14, NIV).
- "We were buried with Him through baptism into death, that just as Christ was raised from the dead by the glory of the Father, even so we also should walk in newness of life" (Rom. 6:4).

- "You died, and your life is hidden with Christ in God" (Col. 3:3).
- "I have been crucified with Christ; it is no longer I who live, but Christ lives in me" (Gal. 2:20).
- "May I never boast except in the cross of our Lord Jesus Christ, through which the world has been crucified to me, and I to the world" (Gal. 6:14, NIV).
- "Sin shall not have dominion over you, for you are not under law but under grace" (Rom. 6:14).
- "You have been regenerated (born again), not from a mortal origin (seed, sperm), but from one that is immortal by the ever living and lasting Word of God" (1 Pet. 1:23, AMPC).
- "If anyone is in Christ, he is a new creation; old things have passed away; behold, all things have become new" (2 Cor. 5:17).
- "There is therefore now no condemnation to those who are in Christ Jesus" (Rom. 8:1).
- "The law of the Spirit of life in Christ Jesus has made me free from the law of sin and death" (Rom. 8:2).
- "If the Spirit of Him who raised Jesus from the dead dwells in you, He who raised Christ from the dead will also give life to your mortal bodies through His Spirit who dwells in you" (Rom. 8:11).
- "For as in Adam all die, even so in Christ all shall be made alive" (1 Cor. 15:22).
- "If we died with Him, we shall also live with Him" (2 Tim. 2:11).
- "We have been made holy through the sacrifice of the body of Jesus Christ once for all" (Heb. 10:10, NIV).
- "In Him dwells all the fullness of the Godhead bodily; and you are complete in Him" (Col. 2:9–10).
- "We are children of God, and if children, then heirs—heirs of God and joint heirs with Christ" (Rom. 8:16–17).
- "You, however, are not in the realm of the flesh but are in the realm of the Spirit, if indeed the Spirit of God lives in you" (Rom. 8:9, NIV).

- "Whoever is united with the Lord is one with him in spirit" (1 Cor. 6:17, NIV).
- "God . . . made us alive together with Christ . . . and raised us up together, and made us sit together in the heavenly places in Christ Jesus" (Eph. 2:4–6).

AN EXHORTATION FOR HEALING BASED ON PSALM 103:1–5

CHAPTER 7 INCLUDES A GUIDED exhortation for healing that Neville wrote in an email. I thought it would be helpful to have it available separately as an appendix, so I've included it here, reformatted and slightly edited. I'm prefacing it with the Scripture on which it is based.

> Bless the LORD, O my soul;
> And all that is within me, bless His holy name!
> Bless the LORD, O my soul,
> And forget not all His benefits:
> Who forgives all your iniquities,
> Who heals all your diseases,
> Who redeems your life from destruction,
> Who crowns you with lovingkindness and tender mercies,
> Who satisfies your mouth with good things,
> So that your youth is renewed like the eagle's. (Ps. 103:1–5)

❦

Please read and meditate on Psalm 103. You will notice that it addresses "all that is within me."

Take the words of the psalm, turn inwards and speak to all that is within you. To every cell, to every brain cell, to every neurone, every synapse and to every neurotransmitter in your brain.

Yes, command everything that is within you to praise the Lord, for He has forgiven you all your sins and healed all your infirmities. He has healed the infirmities of all that is within you.

Take power and authority in Jesus's name. Take the whole armour of God, and command all that is within you in the words of the psalm.

THE BENEFITS OF SALVATION IN JESUS CHRIST

THIS IS ONE OF THE earliest compilations that Neville gave to me, dating from 19 September 1988. He had typed it out spontaneously on an A4 sheet, summarizing in his own words biblical truths that had ignited within his heart.

I have adjusted some of the punctuation and typography for publication, but the words themselves are exactly as he wrote them decades ago.

❧

1. **Because I accept Jesus Christ** as my Lord and Saviour, *I am baptised into His death and buried with Him.*
2. **Because I am buried with Him**, I also *rise with Him and walk in newness of life. I am born from above;* I am *born again.*
3. **Because I am Born again**—*Born of the Spirit*—Christ lives in me. *I live but not I, Christ lives in me. The life I now live is Christ living in me.*
4. **Because Christ lives in me**, I am a *co-heir with Him, I am a child of God.*
5. **Because I am a child of God**, *I am no longer under the dominion of sin, I have been delivered from the law of sin and death* and *I am under the law of Grace.*
6. **Because I am under the law of Grace**, my *inheritance is from God.*
7. **My inheritance [all to the power of n]:**
   a. Salvation
   b. Righteousness
   c. Truth and Wisdom
   d. Life—in abundance, resurrected

e. Power

f. Supply

g. Love—gentleness, meekness, patience

h. Joy

i. Peace

j. Wholeness, healing

ALSO BY ANN SHAKESPEARE

God's Gift of Tremendous Power (Deep River Books, 2019)

Additional Articles and Teachings

nevillejayaweera.com

annshakespeare.com

Upcoming Publications

Ann is preparing a collection of Neville Jayaweera's teachings to be released soon. In addition, she continues to write articles to inspire and encourage faith in Jesus Christ; these are freely available on her website. Learn more about Ann and Neville's writings at the links above, or contact her at info@annshakespeare.com.

Printed in the United States
by Baker & Taylor Publisher Services